D.O.Moberg

DEC 05 1975
LINCOLN CHRISTIAN COLLEGE

W9-BMA-556

DISCARDED FROM
THE MILWAUKEE
PUBLIC LIBRARY
NOT FOR RESALE
OR RENT

261-B859   c12
    Brockway Allan
Secular saint
968   4.95
              MILW. PUB. LIBRARY (91)

Are you getting all your library offers you? ---

IN
    Books
      Magazines
        Newspapers
          Pamphlets
            Government Documents
              Pictures
                Maps
                  Phonograph Records
                    Sheet Music
                      Story Hours
PL-8   Information Service

PUBLIC
LIBRARY
SYSTEM
MILWAUKEE

LIBRARY

THE SECULAR SAINT

ALLAN R. BROCKWAY

The Secular Saint

1968
Doubleday & Company, Inc., Garden City, New York

LIBRARY OF CONGRESS CATALOG CARD NUMBER 68-10560
COPYRIGHT © 1968 BY ALLAN R. BROCKWAY
ALL RIGHTS RESERVED
PRINTED IN THE UNITED STATES OF AMERICA
FIRST EDITION

Grateful acknowledgment is made to the following for copyrighted material:

Harcourt, Brace and Co., Inc.: "pity this busy monster,manunkind": Copyright, 1944, by E. E. Cummings. Reprinted from his volume *Poems 1923–1954* by permission of Harcourt, Brace and Co., Inc., and Faber and Faber Ltd.; "dying is fine)but Death": Copyright, 1950, by E. E. Cummings. Reprinted from his volume *Poems 1923–1954* by Harcourt, Brace and Co., Inc.; extracts from "The Hollow Men" and "The Love Song of J. Alfred Prufrock," both from *Collected Poems, 1909–1962* by T. S. Eliot, used with the permission of Harcourt, Brace and World, Inc., and Faber and Faber Ltd., London.

Alfred A. Knopf, Inc.: "Once I Saw Mountains Angry," "There Was a Man with Tongue of Wood," and "If I Should Cast Off This Tattered Coat," from *The Collected Poems of Stephen Crane*, used with the permission of Alfred A. Knopf, Inc.

Louisiana State University Press: *The Insiders* by Selden Rodman, used by permission of the publisher.

McClelland and Stewart Limited: "The Poetic Process," from *A Red Carpet for the Sun* by Irving Layton, published 1959 by The Canadian Publishers, McClelland and Stewart Limited, Toronto, Canada.

The Macmillan Co.: *Letters and Papers from Prison* by Dietrich Bonhoeffer. Copyright © 1967 The Macmillan Co. Used with the permission of The Macmillan Co. and the SCM Press Ltd., London.

McGraw-Hill Book Company: *Understanding Media: The Extensions of Man* by Marshall McLuhan. Copyright © 1964 by Marshall McLuhan. Used by permission of McGraw-Hill Book Company.

New Directions Publishing Corporation: "A Refusal to Mourn the Death, by Fire, of a Child in London," from *The Collected Poems* of Dylan Thomas, copyright 1945 by the Trustees of the Estate of Dylan Thomas; 1952 by Dylan Thomas. Reprinted by permission of New Directions Publishing Corporation, J. M. Dent, and the Trustees for the Copyrights of the late Dylan Thomas.

The Viking Press, Inc.: "We Are Transmitters" and "Song of a Man Who Has Come Through," from *The Complete Poems of D. H. Lawrence*, Volume I, edited by Vivian de Sola Pinto and Warren Roberts. All Rights Reserved. Reprinted by permission of The Viking Press, Inc., Laurence Pollinger Limited, and the Estate of the Late Mrs. Frieda Lawrence.

John Wiley & Sons, Inc.: *The Step to Man* by John R. Platt, used with the permission of the publisher.

All Bible quotations are from *Good News for Modern Man*, a new translation of the New Testament, Today's English Version, copyright American Bible Society, 1966. Used by permission.

D. Mabry

gratis

30 May 1989

79532

FOR

Harry Kiely

John Mote

Forrest Stith

PREFACE

Several years ago, as a denominational chaplain at a state university, I frequently faced the complaint that students who had been affected by the religious activities on campus returned unable to fit into the church from which they came. They wanted to reform it, and when they found they could not, often dropped out entirely. Obviously, the money that particular church was putting into the campus ministry was going down the drain, or, worse, was being used to lead students away from religion.

This problem is shared by almost all campus clergy who attempt to develop an understanding of the Christian faith that makes sense to today's students. But students are not the only ones presently being alienated from the parish church and from organized religion in general. We are all subject to this disease.

The Secular Saint is for those who have the suspicion that God is not dead, but can see no logical alternative. It is also for those who are angered at the clouds currently floating over the theological and ecclesiastical scene, raising doubts where certainties had existed before. In addition, it is for those who have believed that "Christianity is not only for Sunday but for Monday through Saturday, too," yet have really had little notion of what to do about it. The pages that follow, in other words, are for the thoughtful men and women in today's churches, who continue to struggle with Christian faith as a lived reality.

The words "secular" and "saint" are used descriptively and not judgmentally. In the minds of some, "secular" implies everything evil in the world, but as used here it means only "not religious" or, in Dietrich Bonhoeffer's celebrated word, "religionless." Likewise, "saint" is not meant to convey any special position or state relative to those who make bold to adopt it. Instead, it refers to those who have chosen to live with Christ as their Lord, the meaning used all but universally in the New Testament (e.g., Matthew 27:52; Acts 9:13, 32, 41; Acts 26:10; I Corinthians 1:2; II Corinthians 13:13; Philippians 4:22). A Secular Saint, then, is a "religionless Christian," and this book is an effort to paint a word picture of him, in both his individual and corporate life-styles.

Any attempt to credit all those who have contributed to the thought process that has now resulted in *The Secular Saint* would be fruitless, but simple charity demands that I publicly thank my colleagues on the staff of the General Board of Christian Social Concerns of The Methodist Church, several of whom have read various drafts of the manuscript and have provided wisdom, often without direct intention, that has found its way into these pages. The students of the Faith and Culture Institute, Washington, D.C., who have been the sounding board for the ideas I have here set to print, are due a special debt of gratitude. My colleagues on the staff of that Institute, Harry Kiely, John Mote, and Forrest Stith, to whom this book is dedicated, have suffered with me through each conceptual stage and have carefully read and criticized each draft as it appeared. From the day we began the Faith and Culture Institute, in late 1964, these men have worked toward an existential understanding of the life of the Secular Saint and the present necessity for evolution of parish churches into Corporate Saints. The present work genuinely belongs to them.

In addition, I wish to thank Fred Holt, of the Southwest Regional Office of the Office of Economic Opportunity, Howard Harrod, of the Divinity School of Drake University, and Walter Wink, of Union Theological Seminary, for their invaluable criticism of various parts of the manuscript. Mrs. George Iden and Mrs. T. Marie Dean labored long and faithfully at the typewriter, an activity that poor typists such as I cannot appreciate enough.

Washington, D.C.   *Allan R. Brockway*

CONTENTS

I

The Setting

1

The World of the Secular Saint

XIV

pity this busy monster,manunkind,

not. Progress is a comfortable disease:
your victim(death and life safely beyond)

plays with the bigness of his littleness
—electrons deify one razorblade
into a mountainrange;lenses extend

unwish through curving wherewhen till unwish
returns on its unself.
              A world of made
is not a world of born—pity poor flesh

and trees,poor stars and stones,but never this
fine specimen of hypermagical

ultraomnipotence. We doctors know

a hopeless case if—listen:there's a hell
of a good universe next door;let's go

                      e. e. cummings

THE ONLY CERTAINTY today is change. Even death and taxes seem uncertain. Clearly, "change" as a rubric under which to understand ourselves means that things are not the way they once were and, moreover, things in the future will be different from the way they now are. But most of us have difficulty experiencing ourselves in the midst of change. Our lives, after all, change gradually if at all. The change is evident only when we look back far enough—and then we know what a different world is ours today. Even so, the notion that we will be obliged ten years from now to see our present world as archaic is a bit startling if not frightening.

Each of us lives in his own world. Some of us never know the world of the economically and socially destitute; others are ignorant of "charge-account anxiety"; still others know nothing of the "winter-resort crowd" and the "jet set"; many of us find nightclubs to be foreign; others have never known the society that exists only in the intimate circle of friends and family; for some, apartment living is heaven; for others, anything other than the family farm is hell.

When our own world is no longer what we have learned to expect it to be, we experience change; until then the talk about change is abstract. The farmer knows change when he moves to the city. The poor man knows change when he is offered the possibility of full participation in the consumer economy. The worker knows change when his employer replaces him with a machine. The housewife knows change when she decides to get a job.

Change is neither good nor bad, beneficial nor evil. It simply is. The value or disvalue of specific results of change is attached after the fact by those who experience it and/or reflect on it. But the value judgment cannot alter the fact that the world is different from what it once was. The pressing question for men of today, the men I shall call Secular Saints, concerns the way they are to relate to the changed and changing world in which they live.

A World in Transition

A common way of handling the changing world considers it to be transitional, a time between the times. The former time has passed away; a new time is coming. In the meantime we wait, and now is the time of waiting. But if we try to wait until the new time arrives, we will wait till hell freezes over. Every historical period is transitional, and no particular period may be seen for what it is until it is past; even then the judgment may vary.

Today, historical periods come and go faster than they used to. It is possible, therefore, to isolate at least three distinct transitional periods within the twentieth century, which can be identified by three technological innovations: the automobile, atomic power, and space exploration.

Those who were born around the turn of the twentieth century grew up in the age of the automobile. The horseless carriage was still a novelty, but the handwriting was on the wall—an end to one world was on the way; the beginning of a strange new world had arrived. Those who were to live and grow during the early years of the automobile saw the awakening of social conscience and the crusades of the muckrakers to right the wrongs created by the avarice of men in a vast country that had yet to be fully tamed. Though railroads had already crossed the continent, in 1900 the airplane was still a gleam in the eyes of the Wright brothers; superhighways were beyond any man's vision; the magic lantern had yet to become the movie, much less the talking picture; and the idea that one day men, women, boys, and girls would spend hours each day before a box that brought moving, talking pictures into their homes would have been ludicrous.

In terms of ideas and intellect, the age of the automobile was a veritable ferment. A bright new age was on the way. Matthew Arnold had left his legacy in literary criticism and theology, "higher criticism" had torn the Old Testament apart, and the effect of Schleiermacher and Nietzsche and Marx was still to be fully felt in the works of Troeltsch and Harnack. Science, too, had shaken the stable sensibilities of the common man. Though Darwin's work was some fifty years old, its social effects—in such traumatic events as the "monkey trials"—were yet to be fully discerned.

The age of the automobile was, in other words, a most exciting time to be alive. Nevertheless, the intellectual currents that swept the universities and halls of science had little effect on the everyday life of the laborer and businessman and housewife. Their existence was more likely to be consumed with the price of wheat or hogs, the raising of children into the family business, or the gossip of neighbors and friends. In other words, the nineteenth century still lived in the countryside, where Freud was yet to become a household word.

All this was to be changed by the automobile, which brought personal mobility, something that no other age had known. Persons born about 1900 grew into an entirely mobile world that was to allow their sons and daughters to move hundreds of miles away from the family homestead, if, indeed, the parents did not do so themselves.

Mobility brought its own anxieties. It allowed people to learn that the family farm was not the only way of life available, that people lived and thought differently in different places. It made travel a way of life that one could take for granted. And it also built into its participants the awareness that the life they then knew could actually, not merely theoretically, be other than it was. The automobile gave every man an escape hatch from his present existence.

At the same time, the automobile created its problems, particularly for those born at least thirty years before the advent of the twentieth century. The old story about the newfangled gasoline-powered vehicle frightening the horses tells the tale of an anguish afflicting men and women who knew only the age of immobility. Horses had, in their day, been a radical innovation. After all, the man with a horse could traverse many more miles per day than the man on foot. But horses allowed men to move, basically, only more rapidly over the ground they would have normally traveled on foot. The automobile allowed them actually to go places they would never have gone before. It made them socially free; it changed the shape of society. And it set the stage for the generation that was to come, the generation that was to live in the age of atomic power.

The sons and daughters of the automobile age were born, about 1930, into a period yet to be shaped by the advent of the atomic bomb. While their parents were still young, the Great Depression dashed the great hopes and expectations of the inevitable progress the Enlightenment had produced. The Great War had come and gone—and the world was not yet safe for democracy or anything else. While their parents had celebrated the end of the nineteenth century by dancing the flapper dances, they found themselves living, as children, through World War II, not knowing where their fathers had gone or what their mothers did during the day at the defense factory.

Knowing nothing of the preautomobile age, they took mobility for granted. Automobiles became homes, the places where life was to be lived. Dates with boys or girls were trips in cars; real life was lived in an automobile. The airplane had become an extension of the automobile even for those who had never been near an airport. It was now possible for anyone to go anywhere he chose to go; the only problem was money—and that was often easy to find, particularly if the desire to find it was sufficiently great.

The heightened mobility of the period was evident in ways other than transportation. Colleges were filled with the older young men who had fought in the second World War, and with them came a seriousness for study and personal advancement previously little known in centers for higher education. Gone entirely were the raccoon coats and empty goldfish bowls of earlier days. The seriousness was not entirely due to the more mature student, however. Its roots were set in the two overarching facts of the time: the atomic bomb and the cold war, each of which complemented the other.

The horror of mass destruction in two Japanese cities, Hiroshima and Nagasaki, was a horror that sank into the minds and hearts of the generation born about 1930. And as the United States and the Soviet Union raced each other in the development and construction of ever more devastating weapons of such destruction (the atomic bomb was now obsolete; in its place was the hydrogen bomb and beyond that who knew what), the atomic generation could with little difficulty see the mushroom cloud above their own heads. Thus, the instrument for personal mobility willed them by their parents became an avenue for attempted escape from the terror that was the hallmark of their own time.

But their aimless driving about failed to obscure the threat of total destruction, for the character of the destruction was new, not only to those growing to adulthood, but to all men. For the first time in the history of mankind, the means existed, not only for a tribe or nation to be obliterated, but for man himself to vanish from the earth at a single push of a button. Whereas the automobile age had experienced the necessity of adjusting to new ways, which often brought new promise as well as loss of established patterns, the age of 1930's children was faced with no promise at all. Somehow, the talk about the great technological progress to be realized through atomic power put to peaceful purposes failed to countermand the example of Hiroshima. The road ahead led to nowhere.

"Meaninglessness" was a word that caught the mood of the late 1940's and the following decade. Life had no point when its end was a boom and a cloud, and the period to many seemed less a transition than a genuine end-time: the existence of the Bomb made the actuality of the Bomb-drop a certainty; the only question was when. Lines from the early poems by T. S. Eliot became part of the common parlance: "We are the hollow men/We are the stuffed men/Leaning together/Headpiece filled with straw. Alas!"[1] "In the room the women come and go/Talking of Michelangelo."[2] And J. D. Salinger's restless teen-ager in *The Catcher in the Rye*, Holden Caulfield, became the prototype for an entire generation: everyone who was part of the automobile age was automatically "phony." Facing the end of the world, the past became an unnecessary burden and the future a nonentity; the present was all. At the end of the fifties, Nevil Shute's *On the Beach*, made into a motion picture, brought the whole tenor of the times together. The question, so the movie told its viewers, was how a man was to live facing the inevitable certainty of an atomic death.

Just as the 1930 babies, grown to adulthood, took the automobile for granted, so the babies born about 1945, now coming into full adulthood themselves, took the Bomb for granted; they had never known anything else. And, what is more, the memory of World War II was secondhand to them. In most cases, their fathers had known it only as youths, and to their sons it was simply ancient history, to be studied along with the Peloponnesian Wars as a subject in school. This generation reaped the benefits of that which preceded it in several ways. The Bomb had not fallen and the cold war between the United States and Russia had become more economic than military. Indeed, Russia and the United States were finding common cause because of the rise of mainland China and the developing nations of the "third world." The Bomb, rather than something to fear as imminent tragedy, had become the factor that kept the world more or less at peace: balance of terror can be a good thing. While local wars, such as Korea and Vietnam, seemed certain to keep breaking out in various spots over the globe, the threat of a worldwide conflict seemed increasingly remote.

The principal fact of the time was also a legacy from the previous generation: space exploration. For the first time, men had developed the technology to break loose from the earth's gravity and move into the great unknown that lay beyond the limits of Mother Earth in body as well as through the eye of telescopes, optical and radio.

The scientific and technical breakthrough symbolized a spiritual breakthrough for the space-age generation. The despair and meaninglessness of their elder brothers was lost in the past along with the two great wars; before them stretched the future to be conquered. Equality and justice were now more important than psychological significance, concerns that broke into history in the civil-rights movement, begun in the South by student groups and spreading to all parts of the nation as Negroes and their friends became aware that the injustice of the past was literally that: injustice of the past. The conflict of generations that resulted, although expected, was painful to everyone involved. Nevertheless, the active, militant children of 1945 often found far more personal significance languishing in Southern jails than anyone had ever found in the doleful lines of "The Hollow Men." The day of the martyr had returned.

Instead of asking, "Where can I find meaning in life?", now the question, more embodied than verbalized, was "Into what cause can I throw myself?" The difference in the questions is the difference between the introspective, hopeless 1950's and the action-oriented, impatient, hopeful, and even angry 1960's.

In one of his last essays, Paul Tillich recognized the importance of space exploration on the changing character of our world. "The image of the man who looks down at the earth, not from heaven, but from a cosmic sphere above the earth," he wrote, "became an object of identification and psychological elevation to innumerable people."[3] The truth of Tillich's observation came home to Americans when three astronauts died in an intense fire in their space capsule while practicing for an orbital mission. Somehow, these deaths carried a significance that was not attached to the earlier deaths of other astronauts in a normal airplane crash. When men actually die in the process of space travel, the investment of all men in their endeavor becomes almost too painful to bear.

Tillich noticed another consequence of space exploration. It is "a kind of estrangement between man and earth, an 'objectification' of the earth for man, the depriving 'her' of her 'motherly' character, her power of giving birth, of nourishing, of embracing, of keeping for herself, of calling back to herself. She becomes a large, material body to be looked at and considered as totally calculable."[4] The children of the space age, indeed, found the earth and everything on it to be far more "objective" than had earlier ages. The pragmatism that emerged in the Renaissance and was enhanced during the Enlightenment came to full flower in the age of space exploration. Justice and equality became tangible realities to be historicized by objective means: legislation in the United States Congress. Later, "peace," relative to the Vietnamese war in particular, achieved almost metaphysical status as the civil-rights movement moved into a broader phase. Finally, poverty (a term that remained ambiguous—at what income level did a man or family live in poverty?) became symbolically objective as the federal government attempted to eradicate it in favor of the American symbols for full humanity: money, leisure, and security. All of life was objective for those born about 1945.

Lest I be misunderstood, I should hasten to note that there were many in each transitional period who did not participate in what I have tried to denote as the spirit of the age. Many who were born into the automobile age never lived in it. Instead, they remained throughout their lifetime in the age of immobility to which they were introduced by their parents. Likewise, many who grew into the atomic age never really lived in it, and thousands of young men and women refused to participate in the space age, preferring to live in the automobile or atomic age. At the same time, there were those who, born into the automobile age, found they could be a complete part of the space age. In sum, participation in the current transitional period had nothing to do with chronological age. It had to do with what can only be called spirit identification.

A Steady-State World

Transitional periods nip at each other's heels so quickly that the very term, "transitional period," is fast becoming obsolete. We are now entering a period that can be called "stable" in the sense that men and women no longer experience the social shock that characterized the automobile, atomic, and space ages. The period upon us is the age of the stable change. Man has now reached the point at which nothing shocks him anymore. I do not mean to suggest that his moral sensibilities are not shocked—an insensitivity that has been approached by some in our time—but that change in his physical and social structure no longer causes him to question the value of the world around him or his own worth within it. I am convinced by John R. Platt when he argues that we are now approaching a "steady-state" society, which he believes to be "something rare in the history of the world."[5]

"Will it all be static in this strange new world of the steady state?" Platt asks. "The answer is no, nothing will be static. What will begin to be steady is our acceptance of these new ways of creative leisure and interaction as being the most interesting and most satisfying ways of life."[6] The cliché with which this chapter began —the only certainty is change—points to the essential character of the age into which we are moving today. Change is no longer causing the social and psychological disruption it once produced. In other words, the observation by Marshall McLuhan that "It is change itself, when it occurs very quickly, that creates the misery of psychic alienation"[7] is becoming a truism of the past. Change, even very rapid change, is being assimilated by contemporary men and women with a facility that would have been extremely puzzling, to say the least, to people only a few generations ago.

Once more, it would be ridiculous to suggest that *all* people today accommodate to change without anxiety. Very many do not—but this fact in no way alters the general reality. Platt believes that "in 30 or 40 years, if we survive, the human race will come through this time of wobbling conflict and uncertainty and falling, and will suddenly be riding in its own chosen direction, free, as only a coordinated and confident organism can be."[8] I am inclined to think that the majority of us will have reached this condition much sooner; many are living there now. It is a bit difficult, in fact, to keep in mind the fact that Dietrich Bonhoeffer actually wrote the following words in 1944: "The world that has become conscious of itself and the laws that govern its own existence has grown self-confident in what seems to us to be an uncanny way. False developments and failures do not make the world doubt the necessity of the course that it is taking, or of its development; they are accepted with fortitude and detachment as part of the bargain, and even an event like the present war [World War II] is no exception."[9]

Though born into the automobile age, Bonhoeffer never really lived there. From the heart of a Nazi concentration camp, seeing no end to the most terrible war ever to ravage the earth, he jumped over the anxious atomic age that was to follow his own and came down in the space age, if not the steady-state world of tomorrow's today. "The ordinary man, who spends his everyday life at work and with his family, and of course with all kinds of diversions," he wrote, "is not affected. He has neither the time nor the inclination to concern himself with his existential despair, or to regard his perhaps modest share of happiness as a trial, a trouble, or a calamity."[10] It may be that this "ordinary man" is simply naïve, that he just does not tie in with things as they really are and therefore could not be expected to have the problems—or the rewards—of the more alert, perhaps better-educated man. Something like this could very well be, but it might equally be the case that the ordinary man has always been closer to the steady state than have the direct shapers of any given society. I have no desire to romanticize the ordinary man, but simply to suggest that his stance is now beginning to converge with that of science, technology, philosophy, literature, and art. Technicians have developed transistors to replace vacuum tubes in radios and television receivers and have made insulation-covered wires obsolete by printing the circuits. A name given instruments made with these devices, instruments that are used daily by millions of "ordinary men," is "solid state."

Much has been made of Bonhoeffer's discussion of "worldliness," by those who find it threatening, those who find it wrong, and those who accept it with glee. But it remains an excellent description of the style of life lived by those who inhabit the steady-state world: "By this-worldliness I mean living unreservedly in life's duties, problems, successes and failures, experiences and perplexities."[11] I shall suggest that the man who lives in this way in the steady-state world is the Secular Saint who is enabled to do so through his allegiance to Jesus Christ. But that must remain until later. A discussion of the Christian faith in the steady-state world will intervene, and before that we must look more closely at this strange new world, which is urban, leisurely, external, and religionless.

An Urban World

The urbanity of contemporary society is now old hat to most of us, a fact we take for granted. People and more people live in cities, closer and closer together. Every new census reveals that the population of the rural areas is decreasing rapidly as the population of the cities grows. Cities have spread over the countryside so that the word "city" is no longer adequate to describe them; they are now "megalopoles."

Projections of population increase suggest that by the end of the twentieth century the entire earth could be one giant megalopolis, with a minimum of open space on which to construct synthetic food to be consumed by a population in excess of one hundred billion people. Medicine and better nutrition have lengthened the expected life-span, while birth-control methods have yet to make a noticeable dent in the number of babies—who no longer die at birth. These increased billions of people will be urban, as so many of their fathers and grandfathers are today.

During the time of America's growing pains, the present great cities arose at the junction of rivers, beside harbors, and at railroad connection points. Where roads crossed, towns and villages sprang up; every trail led to a hamlet. People lived where other people lived, unless their livelihood was gained from the farm, in which case they lived among the cornfields and grazing land but came to town on Saturday for staple food items, equipment—and conversation. People, it would seem, need to be with people and will often go to some trouble to be with them. There is safety in numbers, too, as the pioneer travelers across the Western plains discovered— one man could shoot while another loaded—and assistance in house building among neighbors became a frontier tradition. Men did not live alone, for very practical reasons.

But things have changed. Now the rivers and harbors have slight impact on the inhabitants of the cities beside them, and trucks and airplanes have diminished the significance of the railroad. Highways go everywhere; they go to the cities, not the other way around. No longer do the neighbors turn out to "raise a barn"; instead, the barn or the house or the supermarket is built by a building contractor who utilizes, for pay, the services of other contractors and laborers, who may live at some distance from the building site. None of these people know each other in any way other than the association of the job—and the ultimate owner or occupant certainly has never seen or heard the names of those who constructed his edifice.

People still need people, but not in the way they did in other periods of history. What is needed today are the *services* of people, not the people themselves. Oh, we still require the conversation that the farmer found on the town square of a Saturday afternoon. But the conversation now is with people chosen because their interests or habits or backgrounds are similar to our own. The communities that formed the basis for existence break down in the city, where the mobility of the automobile age has become social necessity. No one should be surprised that a common complaint of newcomers to the city is its impersonal character. Individuals simply have no need of other individuals in the way that their small-town and rural grandparents did: the social system takes care of their need for food, clothing, and housing. Contacts with the direct purveyors of these commodities are on the basis of the service provided; no one asks for anything else, and would be rebuffed if he did. Those who identify themselves by means of their community relationships naturally find themselves cut off from personal meaning, and desperately cast about for means of reestablishing the old community in the foreign setting. The results are often disastrous for them and for the society in which the effort is made. Pick up any metropolitan newspaper. The stories of juvenile delinquency, adult crime, prostitution, drug addiction, and mental illness will certainly be there.

The very technology that made it necessary for these automobile and atomic age persons to move to the city and there encounter a thoroughly space-age society is beginning to develop methods for circumventing the trauma of change. Sir Herbert Read is correct in declaring that "What is necessary, for our personal and social health, is some method of guiding the destructive energies of man into positive, creative channels, so that no feelings of frustration ensue."[12] This is a big order indeed, but certainly a technology that can produce nuclear reactions and send men to the moon can come up with methods for allowing men and women to live as creative human beings in a changed and changing society! Poverty, for instance, is not now a social necessity as, perhaps, it once was. We now have the means to abolish it from the face of the earth. John R. Platt speaks out of the character of the day into which we are now fully moving when he writes that "We can no longer afford poverty in the world—if we ever could. We can no longer afford ignorance or prejudice or neglect. It is not so much that they are a sign of moral wickedness as that *they are a sign of incompetence in design and administration*."[13] The import of his words would be startling to the man who lived in the automobile age, for he actually suggests that poverty and ignorance are to be overcome by technology, not by community, self-help, and voluntary mutual aid.

But the idea that technology could overcome the alienation of the cities is repugnant to many who can see value only in the work of their own hands. Cities, not to mention assembly lines, do not offer immediate—or even long-range—gratifications to the individual for his effort. They offer team products, but not the satisfaction of working intimately with others to produce a product that is the direct result of each man's contribution. Instead, they allow partial vision and the awareness, sometimes consciously known and sometimes not, that the individual's work affects in some fashion the end product. The individual tends to be lost in the maze.

Strangely enough, however, the individual is the "king" of the urban world. As never before, the individual human being is the basic social unit. In itself, this is a unique development on the historical scene, for the individual in all previous ages was a part of the community or group before he was an individual. Not so today. In the contemporary urban world, the individual is himself responsible for significant involvement with the world about him. He cannot depend upon his work or the community of which he is a part to provide personal and social meaning.

Like it or not, the situation outlined above is the situation of the contemporary man and woman. Even the family of the urban man is no longer a refuge. Politicians may develop entire campaigns on the theme, "Your home is your castle," and thereby gain a great deal of emotional appeal—with those who have not yet learned to live in the space age, much less the steady-state world of tomorrow's today—but they should know that the appeal is to an antiquated understanding of life. The urban man, and increasingly the urban woman, does not find his primary identity in the family, any more than he finds it in his work or his professional associations. In fact, primary identity is itself becoming a meaningless idea. Urban people do not have any particular center of identity, but find themselves involved in many different groups, none of which is able to provide primary identification. Is the job the man (or woman)? He leaves it at the office or factory when the bell rings. Is the civic club the man (or woman)? He makes time for it when other demands are not too great. Is the church the man (or woman)? He attends on Sunday if he is in town and/or feels like it. Is the P-TA the man (or woman)? He pays his annual dues because he thinks he would be letting his children down if he did not. Is the block club the man (or woman)? He goes if nothing else is doing that night. Primary identity is diffused to the point where it becomes meaningless. We now live in an urban world that provides no central point around which everything else revolves; we are individuals as no men have ever been individuals before, a condition that is not likely to change in the foreseeable future.

Marshall McLuhan denominates the world of today and tomorrow "the electric age," attributing to "instant electric speed" virtually all contemporary social alterations. Television in particular is the shaper—if, indeed, not the *maker*—of men's minds. And it is television that is, according to McLuhan, tolling the death knell for the individual. "Radio and TV," he writes, "by creating a speedup in communication, have hastened the individual back into the embrace of the group without any warning or preparation. The opening of the electronic age seals the entire human family into a single global tribe."[14] McLuhan is enamored of the preliterate tribe, for the tribe had not yet learned to break its experience into small, manageable pieces (a facility that arrived with the widespread use of movable type), and related to the world around itself through a combination of the senses, including, particularly, touch. Television, McLuhan declares, is "the extension of the sense of touch, which involves maximal interplay of all the senses. . . . The mosaic form of the TV image demands participation and involvement in depth of the whole being, as does the sense of touch. . . . To the sense of touch, all things are sudden, counter, original, spare, strange."[15]

Individual man, McLuhan believes, came into existence with printing, when experience began to be perceived entirely through the use of a single sense, sight. He makes his point well, and I find myself in general agreement with him. He is likewise convincing when he argues that television and other electric communication media are involving us in a wider variety of experience at a greater depth. As a result of television we are beginning to *feel* our world, to participate in events that transpire thousands of miles away, to enter into the lives of people whose hands we will never shake. The initial confusion most of us experience when reading that TV is an extension of the sense of touch (after all, don't we *see* and *hear* it?) begins to clarify when McLuhan tells us that "The movie viewer remains quite detached, and is engaged in looking *at* the screen. The TV viewer *is* the screen."[16] A moment's reflection reveals that he is exactly right. Unlike the motion-picture image, which is projected onto the *screen* where we watch it, the television image is projected out of the TV tube onto the *viewer*, who actually becomes part of the communication process. McLuhan makes good sense when he suggests that this medium is altering, if it has not already altered, the perceptual and therefore the social character of contemporary human beings.

When he insists, however, that electric media move us in the direction of retribalization, he fails to understand (or, more charitably, fails to differentiate between an analogy and a reality) the fact that twentieth-century men cannot possibly return to the intimate community relationship patterns that provided life meaning for tribal man. He fails, in other words, to take the symbolic nature of the modern city and the contemporary megalopolis into account. Sociology as well as communication theory and technique shapes mankind. McLuhan's problem stems from what Richard Kostelanetz observes is a "dialectical vision of history by continually referring to pre-print experience (thesis) for his images of the present and future (synthesis) that contrasts with the age of print (antithesis)."[17] But, unlike a pure dialectic, McLuhan's places far greater weight on the thesis, pre-print experience, than on the antithesis, the age of print. In fact, the tone of his work leads the reader to suspect that he is actually antagonistic to the print era and to the human being it produced. This latter he calls "abstract Individual Man" in a paragraph that reveals he is working with a stereotyped image of the individual throughout, and is not in reality suggesting a return to the tribe pure and simple: "The Western way of life attained centuries since by the rigorous separation and specialization of the senses, with the visual sense atop the hierarchy, is not able to withstand the radio and TV waves that wash about the great visual structure of abstract Individual Man. Those who, from political motives, would now add their force to the anti-individual action of our electric technology are puny subliminal automatons aping the patterns of the prevailing electric pressures. A century ago they would, with equal somnambulism, have faced in the opposite direction. . . . What is to be thought of people who wish such a return to preliterate ways, when they have no inkling of how the civilized visual way was ever substituted for tribal auditory magic?"[18]

The city is producing an entirely new kind of individual who is liberated from his past (including his community relationships) by the technology he feared was depriving him of all personhood. McLuhan argues, correctly, that mechanization (which he roots in print culture) produced uniform men and women of necessity. The often decried depersonalization of the assembly line, which made one man replaceable by another, like parts in the machine itself, is rapidly becoming a thing of the past. "The entire approach to these problems in terms of uniformity and social homogenization is a final pressure of the mechanical and industrial technology. Without moralizing, it can be said that the electric age, by involving all men deeply in one another, will come to reject such mechanical solutions. It is more difficult to provide uniqueness and diversity than it is to impose the uniform patterns of mass education; but it is such uniqueness and diversity that can be fostered under electric conditions as never before."[19]

Uniqueness and diversity are characteristic of the city, as they never were either of the tribe or of Western civilization to date, and are the distinctive characteristics of the newly emerging individual, the Secular Saint, whose home is the city. The city is more a mentality than it is a place, a mentality that includes openness, receptivity, and permissiveness. Many who live in cities, of course, do not evidence the city mentality, but that is because they have moved to the city in body only. Conversely, many who live beyond the reaches of megalopolis are full participants in the urban world. It may be, moreover, that the cities themselves are becoming the last refuge of the rural, tribal mentality. Increasingly it is difficult to escape the city's technology on the farm. Not only have the farms become larger and more like industry, but the rural people, unable to adjust to the change in agriculture (as a result of economic deprivation or unwillingness to accommodate to the new technology), have transported themselves and their families to the urban slums. For several years I lived on the Texas high plains, where wheat is the dominant industry. Industry is the appropriate word, for those who engaged in it could scarcely be called farmers in the traditional sense. Near the beginning of the planting season, these manufacturers of foodstuffs climbed on their huge tractors that pulled a bevy of cultivators, and plowed their fields days quicker than their fathers had done the same job with horses and smaller machines. Come seeding time, many of them mounted their airplanes, or hired others to do so, and flew low over the fields, scattering seed behind them. And, when harvesttime came, armies of air-conditioned combines marched through the acres of ripe grain, "bringing in the sheaves." Never did the "farmer" touch the ground. The entire operation could have been performed in a business suit.

This illustration, granted, is an instance of high development of the mechanization that McLuhan decries, but it is a development that has changed the nature of agriculture far beyond the wildest dream of the first users of tractors. It is, furthermore, a development that is utilized by *rural* men, who travel as much as their city cousins, who view as much television, who subscribe to the New York *Times*, and who are often deeply involved in politics. There is no hiding place from the city—unless it is the city itself, where "ghetto" is still appropriate to describe ever larger areas in the heart of America's most urban complexes.

Whatever we may say about it, the fact remains that the steady-state world of tomorrow's today is urban, and probably will be for as long as anyone cares to imagine.

A Leisure World

What we now call leisure—for lack of a better term only—is on the increase. "Discretionary time" would be a more descriptive term, but is too clumsy for ordinary use. Our expanding vocabulary will doubtless come up with a proper word, but until it does we must continue to use "leisure," which came from the day when life was understood primarily in terms of work. The so-called Protestant ethic—if you don't work you don't eat—assumed that each person was responsible to the whole society for his contribution to the common good. His return from the common store was, therefore, to be determined on the basis of his contribution. We have now reached the point, however, at which a contribution is simply not needed from each individual for the society to function at peak efficiency. Human beings are becoming redundant.

Science-fiction writers are not looking too far ahead when they write of future archaeologists coming upon cities that are still functioning, although all the people who once lived in them are dead and gone. Nevil Shute caught this spirit in a terrifying fashion when he depicted, in *On the Beach,* a San Francisco devoid of living persons that nevertheless still sent out telegraphic sounds. John R. Platt puts the issue in a few succinct words: "The problems produced by the elimination of labor are not the problems of the 30 hours a week, or 10 hours, or none, that a man works. They are problems of coupling this to economic distribution and to self-respect, and problems of idleness and boredom in the 138 or 158 or 168 hours when he does not work. They are not nearly as different from the present situation as it is different from that of the last century; and the time when we will be forced to find some kind of solution to these problems is almost certainly within the next decade or two. On the scale of history, are we not almost there already?"[20]

We are indeed. But "problems of idleness and boredom" are almost always problems we imagine rather than problems we actually face. Not many of us actually are faced with these problems today. Most professional people, in fact, do not have sufficient time to do what they have set for themselves, and much less do they have "time on their hands." Even the poor, who are thought by some to be loafing on the welfare rolls, are not idle: their time is consumed with efforts to secure enough food to eat and enough money to pay the extremely high rents exacted by the slum landlord. Idleness and boredom is not our problem; it is a bit strange that we should fear that it might be. The most wished-for state used to be that of the idle rich, who were idolized at the same time they were held in some scorn by the majority of the population. But the idle rich were never oppressed by idleness and boredom. Instead, they seemed to be able to avail themselves of the cultural advantages to which their wealth entitled them: travel, art, literature, and devotion to causes.

We are now faced with the historical anomaly of the idle rich being the common man. The professional and academic classes now spend more hours than there are in the day at their assigned tasks, while the factory worker has fewer compulsory work obligations. This situation will last only one generation, if that long, however. The next generation will contain no factory workers. Factory workers will be as remote as chimney sweeps are today. The steady-state world is a leisure world.

A comic-strip gag has an elderly couple, stopped for a speeding violation and asked where they are going, say, "We're escaping from Leisure World." No one needs have the cartoon explained to him, for everyone knows about the homes for the aged that have sprung up in all parts of the nation. They are, in the main, places for the elderly to while away their time, waiting for death. Society as a whole has no idea what to do with old people, so it puts them away in ghettos, hoping not to have to see them, much less have significant relationships with them. The Leisure Worlds exist because the elderly, who are without work (and it is to our shame that, in a work-oriented society, we have systematically denied them the symbol of value that work provides), would otherwise constantly remind us that leisure is a vital characteristic of the steady-state world.

The prospect of leisure threatens many people because they have not yet realized that there is no such thing as unoccupied time. We are constantly active at something, be it our job, where we earn our living, or play, which we work in order to be able to do, or even sleep. I seriously question the notion that, were men not required to work, they would do nothing but sit around twiddling their thumbs (or some other image that connotes total inactivity), being lulled into no-humans by television. Certainly this latter idea has been thoroughly discredited by McLuhan, who demonstrates that television, far from numbing men's sensitivities, heightens them. Perhaps, sitting around all day watching television would be the best thing that could happen to any of us!

The real problem with the leisure of the steady-state world is what Platt called the coupling of leisure to "economic distribution and to self-respect." Work at the present time is simply not related directly to income. We have only to think of the millions of housewives who spend hours daily at what most of us could only call hard labor, but who receive not one penny for their efforts. I have mentioned this fact in discussion groups on occasion, only to be answered by the serious student or housewife: "Yes, but she is related to a person (her husband) whose income and work are related. If she wasn't taking care of the home and children, he would have to hire someone to do it. She is actually very valuable." The answer is, of course, partially correct. The housewife is tremendously valuable —but not because she works. Because she is wife to a breadwinner, however, in no way alters the fact that *her* work does not directly produce economic gain.

The housewife may not have major difficulties relative to self-respect, however. The reason for this good fortune lies in the tradition that it is not the individual but the family unit which must have direct work-income correspondence. As long, therefore, as she is part of such a family unit, her labor remains part of the cooperative effort which allows her husband to leave the house each day to engage in activity for which he receives a periodic paycheck. Only when there is no family member who "works" does housewifery become socially degrading.

Other categories of Americans also participate in economic structures that provide them the ability to participate in the consumer economy without direct contribution on their part. Among them are the millions who live on income from investments, life insurance, and pensions. Their efforts do not produce this income; the rejoinder that they, or someone, worked for this money is beside the point—at the present time their activity is not related to their economic position. The same is true of very highly paid executives and scientists. How could any man possibly be worth, in terms of his daily production, in excess of $500,000 annually? When you get right down to it, what objective standard of measurement exists for evaluating the economic worth of a human being and his activity? I am suggesting here that in our steady-state world it is simply not a fact that income and productivity are directly related—already. Our job system is a means for distributing the corporate wealth, a system that has worked more or less effectively since the Renaissance. (In most cases, it has worked less rather than more effectively.)

In a technological society that is rapidly dispensing with the necessity for jobs, new and different methods must be devised for distributing the wealth. Proposals for such methods usually are labeled "income maintenance" or "guaranteed income" programs, to be funded through the federal government. These proposals have encountered the same objections to which public welfare has long been subject (guaranteed income is not welfare). How could a man respect himself if he received money from the government or anyone else without working for it? The answer may lie in the suggestion, made by many economists and philosophers today, that people be paid, throughout their lifetime, to learn—simply for the sake of learning, of expanding their sensibilities, and not in order to do something with their increased knowledge later. In the steady-state world of tomorrow's today, men will be free to do what they choose to do, not what they are compelled to do. Learning is the process of choosing to live free.

The technology of our world, by releasing men from the necessity to spend their lives at a job, is freeing them to search for and to create the unique, to take delight in thought, in creation, even in passivity. And this is what learning is all about. McLuhan captures the essence of the new leisure world for us all when he says that "The very same process of automation that causes a withdrawal of the present work force from industry causes learning itself to become the principal kind of production and consumption. Hence the folly of alarm about unemployment. Paid learning is already becoming both the dominant employment and the source of new wealth in our society. This is the new *role* for men in society, whereas the older mechanistic idea of 'jobs,' or fragmented tasks and specialist slots for 'workers,' becomes meaningless under automation."[21]

An External World

The age of the atom was an internal age, which saw the full flowering of the psychiatric and psychoanalytic movements. During this time, the headshrinker (often affectionately so called even by his patients) became the panacea for thousands of men and women who could see no way beyond the personal, social, and political impasse in which they found themselves. During this time mental illness began to lose its stigma—a process that, unfortunately, is yet to be completed—and having been in analysis became a status symbol among some groups, a development that was not hindered by the high cost of psychoanalysis and the scarcity of doctors qualified to perform this service. The period was characterized by a careful searching of the interior of men's minds for the meaning, not only of their own lives, but of the universe itself.

I have already mentioned the emphasis among college students upon the poetry of T. S. Eliot and their identity with Holden Caulfield. In the first instance, students found an accurate reflection of their own perception of the world around them. Everything was indeed hollow and meaningless. And, although the reasons lay in the general breakdown of the stable universe that, most of them believed, had existed prior to the two World Wars, they nevertheless were ridden with guilt at not being able to find some sort of meaning within themselves. Thus, the general anxiety of the day combined with a residual guilt, whose roots lay in the Protestant ethic, to produce an entire generation that withdrew from society. During this time the theological and social works of Walter Rauschenbush, written just prior to 1920, fell into almost total eclipse, and the early works of Reinhold Niebuhr, written only a little more than a decade later, became popular. Sin and guilt once more were at the forefront of both social and theological thinking. The problem was to overcome internal alienation which, projected, became alienation between the person and his environment, not to mention everything in general. It was Paul Tillich who, in *The Shaking of the Foundations*, gave explicit intellectual and theological shape to the internal mood. Sin, he said, was alienation between oneself and oneself, between oneself and others, and between oneself and the Ground of Being. His answer was "Simply accept the fact that you are accepted," and it was an answer that spoke profoundly to many a person.

But the steady-state world is not the atomic age, or even the space age into which the internal emphasis extended. The steady-state world is external, because the personal and social conflict caused by rapid change is no longer with us: we expect change and even anticipate it with pleasure. In that kind of world a man looks outside himself, not inside. "After the shock-front has passed, we will have reached larger powers and inter-actions—higher temperatures and pressures—but . . . the buffeting of change will be reduced, and the times will perhaps become psychologically and socially calmer than anything this generation or this century has known."[22]

Speaking of the university student of 1967, Paul Goodman rightly suggests that "The shagginess and chosen poverty of student communities have nuances that might be immensely important for the future." This student generation, he says, "are the young of the affluent society, used to a high standard of living and confident that, if and when they want, they can fit in and make good money. Having suffered little pressure of insecurity, *they have little psychological need to climb:* just as, coming from respectable homes, they feel no disgrace about sitting a few nights in jail. *By confidence they are aristocrats—en masse.* This, too, is unique in history."[23]

The steady-state world into which we are moving is populated by people who have no psychological need to make something of themselves—because they will have the social and economic assurance they need as an accepted right in society, an assurance that will not depend upon large participation in the affluent society (a term that is already beginning to lose its sense; when all men in the world are affluent, it is not necessary to speak of affluent societies). The new world is populated by aristocrats, no one else, who are free to direct their attentions to persons, events, and objects outside their own private world.

Before anyone discounts the sentences above as being hopelessly utopian, let us quickly remind ourselves of the students, the housewives, the corporation executives, the entertainers, and many others who *now* enjoy complete economic security, a security marred only by the possibility that it might be taken away if they are not careful. The absence of this fear awaits only the establishment of a substantial program of income maintenance—which almost certainly will become a reality within the next ten years. But, then, if the steady-state world be utopian, let it be so. As Platt says, "The world has now become too dangerous for anything less than Utopia."[24]

What makes our new world so tremendously exciting is its liberating quality, which both Platt and McLuhan detail. The freedom comes, in large measure, from the technological environment itself. Erich Fromm has pointed out that "Whether or not the individual is healthy is primarily not an individual matter, but depends on the structure of his society. A healthy society furthers man's capacity to love his fellowmen, to work creatively, to develop his reason and objectivity, to have a sense of self which is based on the experience of his own productive powers."[25] Fromm concludes that "society can further man's healthy development, and it can hinder it; in fact most societies do both, and the question is only to what degree and in what directions their positive and negative influence is exercised."[26] I cannot agree with the prognosis Fromm and others have offered, that our society is hard down the road to sickness, which will produce more and more depersonalized people. Instead, I am convinced that history has now presented us with the possibility—which is being actualized—of changing the environment in such fashion that the individual may be free from the harassing dreads he thought were part and parcel of the human condition. Kostelanetz notes that McLuhan predicts "that as changing society becomes more sympathetic to the human essence, most anxiety and neurosis will disappear,"[27] an insight I have already noted is present in Platt as well.

Paul Goodman is the current darling of the campus radicals. He dresses the part and his life-style is free in the way they like to think theirs is, too. For his own part, Goodman believes he has an inside track to the contemporary student mind, which he probably does. For this reason, he is a man to take seriously when he talks about the young people who will shape the steady-state world. "In their own action programs [directed outward] the young are almost fanatically opposed to top-down direction. . . . In imitating Gandhian nonviolence, they do not like to submit to rigid discipline, but each one wants to make his own moral decision about getting his head broken. . . . By such means they will never get power. But, indeed, they do not want power, they want meaning."[28]

If we take this statement as valid, we can see that what Platt called the "shock-front" is still in process of passing. Anybody who is still looking around for *meaning* does not live in the steady-state world. In truth, none of us do right now, but that world is the real world of the Secular Saint, the hero of this book. It is a world we must learn to live within now if we are genuinely to live in it when it fully arrives.

One of the signs of the steady-state world is the preeminence of large organizations, be they governmental or otherwise. Organizations operate on an objective basis; what is good is what makes money for the corporation, what can be passed through Congress, what can crack the problem of cancer. Organizations seldom take personal consideration into account; when they do they tend to become ineffectual. In other words, organizations are externally oriented. More than *twenty years* ago, Dietrich Bonhoeffer wrote that "our immediate environment is not nature, as formerly, but organization."[29] In his moving essay, "Thoughts on the Baptism of D.W.R.," he asked, "Are we moving towards an age of colossal organizations and collective institutions, or will the desire of innumerable people for small, manageable, personal relationships be satisfied? Must they be mutually exclusive? Might it not be that world organizations themselves, with their wide meshes, will allow more scope for personal interests?"[30]

The answer, two decades later, is a clear yes. Through large organizations, including a worldwide government, the individual—you and I—is set free to choose the involvements he wishes, to choose the style of life that suits him best. The world of the Secular Saint is a world free of internal anxieties and internal solutions to problems. It is a world in which we will be free to push out to the limits of our relationships, to be (in a very fine sense) other-directed.

A Religionless World

The steady-state world is bereft of religion. No one should be surprised at this statement, for religion has always been a device for allowing men and women to live in a world that is antagonistic to them. The world of the Secular Saint is not this kind of world. "But religion is an integral part of life; no man can live without some kind of religion. Didn't Tillich say that religion is a part of our cultural life?" He did indeed, but he is no longer correct. Men who live in the steady-state world have no need for religion. Religion, no matter how conceived, is an effort on the part of its adherents to escape from the world they have on their hands. When life is intolerable, men inevitably search for ways to make it bearable, and otherworldly avenues are by far the easiest.

A premise of traditional Christian religion is that this world is only one of the existing worlds; there is another—the utopia every man longs for—whose name is heaven, and a third—the perverse utopia—whose name is hell. Conduct in the earthly world, the here and now, determines those who are to live in heaven and those who are to live in hell. Those who "act right" get to heaven and, of course, those who don't end up in hell. Sometimes the condition is belief in "the Lord Jesus Christ," sometimes it is allegiance to the church. But whatever the conditions for entrance into heaven, heaven remains as the time and place where it is no longer necessary to perform properly, where leisure or freedom reigns.

It is no longer fashionable to talk much about heaven and hell, because the spatial concepts are meaningless even to very religious people. But the functions performed by these religious realities are still highly desirable to many of us. If we can't have heaven, we still must have some way of understanding the universe and our place in it that takes the misery of the world into account and provides an alternative. But the realization is growing among us that there simply is no world, good or bad, other than the one in which we live. Religion has become something to study in anthropology classes, not something to be lived. And, interestingly enough, this realization has brought us close to the condition we had envisioned heaven to be: the state of no religion at all.

Religion, of course, is more than a metaphysical picture of the universe. It is the belief that something makes life worth the living. In 1943 H. Richard Niebuhr wrote that "no man lives without living for some purpose, for the glorification of some god, for the advancement of some cause."[31] Affirmations such as this one have been taken at face value for too long, and now the common man simply ignores them. In the steady-state world of tomorrow's today, men do live apart from "some purpose," "the glorification of some god," and "the advancement of some cause." We know that Bonhoeffer was right when he wrote on June 27, 1944, "The truth is, we've given up worshipping everything, even idols. In fact, we are absolute nihilists."[32] There is a note of sadness in this statement, as there must always be when something good and highly valued disappears, but the sadness is tempered by the realization that the religionless world is the most exciting world men have ever inhabited, and that God is yet a powerful symbol through which to relate to the steady-state world that is upon us.

II

The Style

2

The Edge Is the Center

A REFUSAL TO MOURN THE DEATH, BY FIRE, OF A CHILD IN LONDON

Never until the mankind making
Bird beast and flower
Fathering and all humbling darkness
Tells with silence the last light breaking
And the still hour
Is come of the sea tumbling in harness

And I must enter again the round
Zion of the water bead
And the synagogue of the ear of corn
Shall I let pray the shadow of a sound
Or sow my salt seed
In the least valley of sackcloth to mourn

The majesty and burning of the child's death.
I shall not murder
The mankind of her going with a grave truth
Nor blaspheme down the stations of the breath
With any further
Elegy of innocence and youth.

Deep with the first dead lies London's daughter,
Robed in the long friends,
The grains beyond age, the dark veins of her mother,
Secret by the unmourning water
Of the riding Thames.
After the first death, there is no other.

DYLAN THOMAS

TO BELIEVE IN is not "to believe that." Therein lies Dick's significance in my life, for Dick brought me face to face with the God I had been professing "belief in" for many years. It was Dick who forced me to understand that I had been saying the Apostles' Creed as though it read, "I believe *that* God the Father Almighty *is* maker of Heaven and Earth." Dick, in other words, confronted me with God himself, not a statement about him. But he had to die to do it.

I had known Dick since early childhood. We came into the world during the same year, if not exactly the same month. We were in the same class at school, where we sat next to one another. We seemed to gravitate toward the same hangouts, found ourselves in basic agreement on the movies to be seen, and even—at different times—dated the same girls. As we grew older, we went to the same college and studied similar subjects, but after college we went our different ways; I to seminary and he to the Navy. We were still single, a condition that was not to remain unchanged for long.

Before the change took place, however, a far more significant alteration was to transpire in Dick's life. I learned of it through mutual friends, who wrote—along with other items of hometown gossip —that Dick had cancer. He was to undergo an operation and the prognosis was hopeful. I was concerned, but, since it seemed reasonable to assume Dick would come through this one as he had other illnesses and injuries, I soon let it slip my mind. In fact, I next thought of Dick when I received another casual note saying he had come through the operation in good order. He was going to be all right.

But the optimism was premature. Only a month or so later Dick appeared at my dormitory door. He was en route to a military hospital where he would have another operation; the tumor had not been entirely removed. He was cheerful and certain this time the matter would be cleared up once and for all.

The next word from Dick came in two envelopes side by side in the same mail. The first brought the message that Dick's cancer was too far gone—he had only a few months, at best, to live. The second, a small, square envelope, held a wedding announcement. Dick had gotten married! When he knew he was going to die! I had just been married myself and had found it traumatic enough, but when you knew for sure that in a few months. . . .

Time wore on, and Dick didn't die. He passed the first deadline and then the second, and my own first child had screamed his first cry when I got the notice of Dick's newborn daughter. I could scarcely believe my eyes. How could he dare to have a child when he knew he was going to die? Yet he did, although the little girl never knew her father: two days later a phone call told me Dick was dead. And I was confronted with God.

Religion is supposed to be a great comfort in the face of death. Religion tells us that anxiety and grief may be relieved, for the formerly living person is actually living still in heaven. (At the time of death no one mentions hell. Those who know of its reality—the grievers—try to pretend it isn't there.) And further, religion tells us that the death is "God's will" and therefore somehow all right. Religion, in other words, tells us that the death the griever faces is either not real or must be stoically accepted as part of a larger scheme of things which, while unknown to living human beings, is fully known to the mind of the Creator, who personally has seen to it that his will is translated into reality. God, in this view, is either the benevolent caretaker of an immense formal garden of eternal life, or the despotic and capricious puppeteer who cuts the human lifeline at will.

But it was not this God who met me in the message of Dick's death. In that event I found myself cheek by jowl, not with an understanding of God's will, but with God himself, not with a far-off deity who controls the universe, but with the very real and present definition of my own life.

What was the actual difference between my life and Dick's? Obviously, he was dead and I was not. But that wasn't all. Looking back at my reactions to the events of those weeks, I began to see clearly that the only difference between us was that Dick had some assurance of *when* he would die. I knew I was going to die, too, yet I dared to be married. I knew I was going to die, yet I dared to have children. The difference was I didn't believe in my own death. He did, and went on living anyhow, in the very face of the concrete limit to his existence. And I began to see that in Dick's death I had met my own limit, began to understand existentially that my life was limited, and that I had to come to terms with that limit, beyond which I could not possibly go.

The Limit and the Demand: God

There is no way of knowing how many different specific items have, through the ages, been given the name God. But whatever it is—rock, animal, sculpture, oblong blur—it is always understood as genuinely external, utterly different, alien to man. It is the activity that says, "Thus far and no farther." It is the limit beyond which man cannot go. Men have seldom been able to determine exactly when or where the limit will appear. But they seldom have much difficulty knowing when it does.

While the absolute limit to a man's life is indeed a border, an impenetrable wall, it does not appear solely on the edge of life, in extreme circumstances. Dick's death was not an extreme situation for me. My own immediate existence was not threatened, as it would be, for instance, by the death of my wife or children. Yet in that event, which took place hundreds of miles from where I lived, came lively knowledge of the definition of my own life, the point beyond which was reality, perhaps, but not *me*.

The limit appears in many forms far less extreme than death. It appears in the breakdown of the automobile when it simply *must* run. It appears in the rejection of a credit application. It appears in the destruction of a treasured heirloom, in the collapse of a carefully developed intellectual framework, in the leveled wheatfield after a hailstorm. In each such case, a man encounters the historical presence that lets him know he is a man.

For, after all, the difference between man and God is man's limits. Man is limited; God is limit. Man is defined; God is definition. But men have never been content with being men, they have never been satisfied with the limits that define them. They have wanted, in other words, to be God.

In that fact lies the difference between a man and a bug. A man knows he is limited and tries to be more than he is. A bug, unaware of his limited existence and its manifestations, runs hither and yon, responding immediately to what it encounters. It is man who lives in the tension between being equally unable to be a bug or to be God. When demands are placed on him that he wishes to avoid, he longs to become a bug. When he is faced with intolerable limitations, he longs to be God. But only very rarely does he wish to be a man.

In both the limitations and the demands, a man is faced with God. Finally, it is God who insists that a man be a man—and not God or a bug. It is God who demands that the center of a man's life be right on the edge, where the danger of bumping into the absolute limit is greatest. It is God who demands that a man face his limits rather than run away from them. It is God who forces a man not to be a bug.

In his demand that a man be a man, God does not only appear as the absolute limit to existence. Often he appears as what requires a man not to place limits upon himself. A man develops a safe way to be God when he circumscribes his life within a narrow compass; he can be both the self-limited man and his limiter, the creator and the created. He sets limits over which he has control, limits that are not limits at all.

To the self-limited man—to the self-elected bug—God comes as the destroyer of false limits. He comes, in other words, as a demand, as a challenge. As such, God is seldom seen as something good, for the bug does not want to risk his secure, self-deified less-than-manhood. He does not want to be forced to risk himself. He does not want to live at the edge of life—it is too frightening out there.

I once knew a woman—let us call her Rhonda—who had worked very hard as an executive secretary. She was quick and efficient. Her employer knew he could count on her to take his most hastily scribbled notes and execute them without fail. She enjoyed her work and took pleasure in the approval of her boss. She was always cheerful. But she did her work too well.

When an opening appeared in the office for an administrative assistant, she was offered the position. It meant a significant increase in salary—an important item, for she had just acquired a set of additional expenses. She jumped at the opportunity, quite flattered to be considered capable of handling the additional responsibility.

But being an administrative assistant involved radically different duties than she had known as a secretary. In her new office, Rhonda was expected to take full responsibility for entire segments of the firm's sales program. She had to make decisions on her own that affected the entire company.

The ready smile and the snappy rejoinder, which had been her trademark in the office, became more rare. Her superior began to notice that she took more sick leave. She began to see a psychiatrist. When asked how she felt, she tended to complain of how tired she was. And, in moments of candor, she was heard to wish she was a secretary again.

Her superior could not understand what had happened to Rhonda. The efficiency he had come to take for granted was a thing of the past. Matters that reached her desk never seemed to leave there. Everything in her employment history had pointed to the fact that she was more than capable of performing her new job well. Why wasn't she?

Rhonda was being faced by the demand to be more than she had defined herself to be. She was confronted by the demand not to be a bug, albeit a happy bug. (Bugs are always happy, but they are also vulnerable.) For the bug, it is a terrible thing to fall into the hands of a great demand. Thus it was with Rhonda. She came face to face with God—and she ran away from him, refusing to live at the edge of her life.

God meets us in the very center of life, at the point where we are most jealous of our own creation. He meets us as the limit where we experience the command, "Thus far and no farther," and he meets us as the demand that requires us to breach our self-imposed limitations. He forces us to assume responsibility for being *men*.

The Stop-Gap God

Why should we call what says no to our aspirations, and yes to the impossible, God? Others have called it Luck or Fate. Still others have called it the Devil or "the way life is." Why should we call it God?

The very fact that this question comes immediately to mind points to the further fact that the question of God is acute for twentieth-century man. Ours is an age that takes some pride in dispensing with God. Liberal churchmen in particular have latched onto Dietrich Bonhoeffer's startling "discovery" of a "world come of age" in which "mature" men do indeed get along "without 'God' and just as well as before." But what God is it the mature man lives without? In a passage ignored by the cliché-makers and sensation hunters, Bonhoeffer made no secret of the neglected God's identity:

> "Weizsäcker's book *Das Weltbild der Physik* is still keeping me very busy. It has again brought home to me quite clearly how wrong it is to use God as a stop-gap for the incompleteness of our knowledge. If in fact the frontiers of knowledge are being pushed further and further back (and that is bound to be the case), then God is being pushed back with them, and is therefore continually in retreat."[1]

What kind of deity is it that can be changed in character and limited in sphere of influence by human knowledge? It is the God that "explains" incomprehensible phenomena. The stop-gap God fills up the space between what man can know and do and absolute truth and goodness, between imperfection and perfection. Those who believe this God is real bring him into the picture when natural catastrophe strikes, for example. Since the wind and rain are uncontrollable by man, they must be controlled by God. So the stop-gap God has taken his place in our legal language. Everyone who has an insurance policy on his home can find in it a phrase that lets the insurance company off the hook in the case of "acts of God."

When a hurricane strikes, killing many people and destroying millions of dollars worth of property, the faithful of the stop-gap God organize their discussion groups and Sunday school classes to discuss "The problem of suffering, or How can a good God allow such destruction and pain?" The answer is usually present from the beginning: there is a higher (i.e., long-range) purpose in it all. We don't know what it is, but God doen't allow these things to happen unless he has an ultimate good in mind. If we wait long enough that purpose will be manifest.

This customary explanation reveals a vital characteristic of the stop-gap God. He is good, i.e., his activity is ultimately designed to effect the "best interests" of human beings. In fact, his only reason for being is to do good things for men. This moral addition to the fundamentally epistemological character of the stop-gap God causes a great deal of confusion, of course. But it is a logical extension of the God who fills the gap between what we know and do not know. But what does "good" mean to the devotees of the stop-gap God? Inevitably it means "pleasurable for me," but since the worshiper cannot allow himself to be "selfish," personal pleasure is projected to a general norm. In the same way, "evil" means "painful for me" and is likewise projected to a general norm.

Since the Renaissance, and particularly since the Enlightenment (in which we still live), knowledge of the world has been held to be beneficial to man. If only he knew enough, there would be no natural catastrophes. Such knowledge would enable man to provide a more beneficial world, a world that would be *good*. But, paradoxically, most followers of the stop-gap God fear knowledge as well: too much knowledge on man's part would threaten the position of God himself. And, of course, they can call the second creation story in Genesis to their aid. But that story serves only to increase the value of knowledge, for knowledge is identified with God and is thus good. The God that is the extension of man's knowledge must, by definition, be good—even though, at first glance, he doesn't always act that way.

Because followers of the stop-gap God know he is good, they cannot permit him to be the *actual* cause of natural catastrophe. He only *allows* it to happen. He could stop it or prevent it if he chose; he just doesn't. Confusion arises when someone dares to ask what lies behind the great wind God doesn't stop. The question is usually sidestepped or ignored in the twentieth century, for we can't talk of devils or demons anymore.

The best way to handle the problem of evil forces is to change the subject from "natural" suffering to suffering at the hands of men, war in particular. The ground is firmer here, for man has a free will that may act contrary to God's will—and God lets man destroy himself if he wants to do so. It is not necessary to have supernatural forces opposing God. Man—a well-known opponent of deity—is capable of it himself. The problem then becomes a simple tactical matter of convincing everyone to adhere to the stop-gap God. When that goal is achieved, all evil will come to an end. The function of the stop-gap God is, therefore, to perfect this as yet imperfect world. But the world stays imperfect and God, the perfect one, stays far away.

It is scarcely any wonder that twentieth-century man gets along without the stop-gap God, who is not to be found in the world (if he could be, he would no longer be God) and is really only a projection of man's own knowledge. Even if a man may believe this God exists, the belief has no practical significance. He cannot live his life on the God's terms. Life is lived in the world, with the knowledge and goodness belonging to man, and modern men know this even when they pretend otherwise to themselves, usually on Sunday.

The Escape-Hatch God

Trained from early childhood to believe that the stop-gap God is real and serviceable to them, modern men may assuage their latent guilt at ignoring him by turning to the stop-gap God's Siamese twin, the escape-hatch God. What the stop-gap God is for the mind, the escape-hatch God is for the emotions. Whereas the stop-gap God perfects the imperfection of the world, the escape-hatch God makes it unnecessary to live in the world at all. He is always ready to hand when everything else fails. When life becomes intolerable, he is there to assure man that it really doesn't matter, for genuine life is in heaven with him. He is the God of salvation—salvation from the "slings and arrows of outrageous fortune."

The escape-hatch God is closer to man than is the stop-gap God. Indeed, he is always at man's side, ready to whisper in his ear that his troubles will all pass away if only he will believe the word of salvation. It is easy for a man to ignore the escape-hatch God when all is going well. In fact, it would seem God would have it so himself—just so long as he is called in when the tide turns. And so he is. The escape-hatch God occupies every foxhole.

But in order for him to be the "ever present help in trouble," the escape-hatch God must be encountered before the trouble comes. He must be known to be available. And, unlike the stop-gap God, he has a tangible manifestation that testifies to his presence. He can be felt.

As a teen-ager, I was an avid devotee of the escape-hatch God. I was, indeed, a most capable priest of this *deus ex machina*. A single incident in that priesthood will serve to illustrate both the power and impotence of the escape-hatch God.

A fellow student was stricken with poliomyelitis, or infantile paralysis, as it was commonly called. Mike was a popular boy at school, a football player, which partly explains the profound concern on the part of his classmates at his illness. He had become sick following a particularly strenuous practice session. Since he was rehearsing to represent the school in the coming game, each of us, as students who identified with the school, was involved. When the local hospital was unable to treat him adequately, Mike was transferred to the state capital, where a special hospital for polio victims had been established. Reports from downstate filtered back: Mike was not doing well. It was time for God to step in.

As chairman of the worship committee of the church youth group, it fell to my responsibility to plan and execute a worship service for Mike on Sunday evening. I arranged the chairs in two concentric circles, located a proper passage of scripture, quickly prepared a talk, and arranged for someone to turn out the lights, leaving only the candles on the altar, when it came time for the prayer.

The service was a great success. My closing prayer for Mike's life was so moving that friends told me it was the best prayer they had ever heard. Afterward, a group of us sat on the steps outside talking about the worship service and about Mike. I had no doubt that Mike would live, and would not have been surprised if he had taken a turn for the better at the very time I had been praying. Then a group of students drove up in an automobile. One stuck his head out the window to inform us Mike had died four hours before.

I was stunned. But my faith was not shaken. We simply had waited too long. If we had only had the worship service in the morning instead of the evening, Mike would still be alive! We—I—had goofed. We had waited too long to get God in on the situation.

The students gathered once again in the youth fellowship room, this time to pray for ourselves, to ask forgiveness of the escape-hatch God for not acting in time. And also, not to be remiss a second time, to pray for Mike's soul, that he would live forever in paradise. In both services there was no doubt of the escape-hatch God's presence. We felt him. Our emotions told us he was very near.

I was naïve then. Sophisticated worshipers of the escape-hatch God would not have put him to the test as I had done. Older and wiser worshipers would have *begun* with prayer for Mike in the abstract, that is to say, for his soul. Then they would have prayed for his recovery, "if it be thy will." Thus, they would have had, as I did not, a way out in the event of Mike's actual death: it simply wasn't God's will that he live.

The escape-hatch God, like the stop-gap God, has a will. And it is not a will that may be magically controlled, as I simply assumed when I prayed for Mike's life. "God's will" is oriented toward man's welfare in the long run. Thus, the one whose will it is that Mike die is the one who stands ready to comfort when death occurs. His assurance is that the loved one has but moved on to a better life. Since it is "God's will," those left behind can only accept it and hope, with God's help, to make the best of it. The comfort of the escape-hatch God feeds back from death into every trying situation in life. The basic message is: the worshiper can take almost anything here and now because eternal bliss is on the way.

The escape-hatch God and the stop-gap God finally merge into each other, for each has nothing to do with the actualities of historical existence. The stop-gap God, filling the space between the known and the unknown, may be part of the unknown but is certainly foreign to the known, for, by definition, he may not enter into history. Precisely the same is true of the escape-hatch God, who, a haven from the slings and arrows of contemporary existence, must of necessity remain remote from daily reality, except as he is constantly present to provide a way out of that very existence which is actual life. Both Gods tend, therefore, to choose the same worshipers, who almost without exception make no distinction between them. They are, for all practical purposes, the same God.

I suggested earlier that the question of God is acute for twentieth-century man. And it is so because men cannot believe *in* the stop-gap and escape-hatch God. They can only believe *that* he exists, much as they believe Mars is a planet of our sun. But men today know they are supposed to believe *in* this God, of whom they have learned since childhood. The conflict is equally great for those who are faithful churchgoers and for those who reject God entirely.

Those who believe that the stop-gap and escape-hatch God exist are of two kinds: (1) those who pretend to themselves and others that they actually believe in him; and (2) those who openly believe only that he exists, and go about their lives without the belief making any appreciable difference. The former are likely to be in great internal conflict unless they have become a bit schizophrenic. The latter are likely not to talk of God or the church at all, and, indeed, avoid it like the plague—for fear their latent guilt may come to the surface.

These more or less faithful followers are caught in an absurd plight, for the God about whom they are anxious is not real and never has been. He is a fabrication of the longings of generations of humans, projected "out there" and given conceptual form. Nothing short of a complete break with this God will be sufficient to release them into genuinely free and meaningful life.

On the other hand, those who completely reject this God are left with the question in Stephen Crane's poem:

> If I should cast off this tattered coat,
> And go free into the mighty sky;
> If I should find nothing there
> But a vast blue,
> Echoless, ignorant—
> What then?[2]

They have indeed shucked off belief *that*. But they still operate within the same frame of reference as those who believe God exists. They have merely turned belief *that* upside down. Thinking the real significance of the word God is what the true believer thinks it is, these negative men allow themselves—often with great bravado—to be labeled atheists, men without God. But what have they gained save a fight—exhilarating perhaps—with the believers?

What is necessary for both believer and unbeliever is a complete alteration of context, an entirely different frame of reference. Instead of asking, "What can God do for me?", or maintaining that one has no need of the very God to whom he is tied in rejection, a new question must be raised: Where does the Christian tradition point in historical existence with the verbal symbol, God?

The believer finds this new question difficult to ask because it would mean giving up his supernatural explainer and comforter. The atheist finds it difficult to ask because to take the question of God seriously would mean giving up his identification as an atheist. For both, the question asks how God himself is encountered, not how his will is discerned. It demands a radical change in context.

A Nondefinition of God

Thus, I return to the question put earlier. Why should we call what says no to our aspirations, and yes to the impossible, God? The answer, of course, is that we have no choice—if we use the word God at all—but to do so, unless we are going to depend upon the stop-gap and escape-hatch God. Yet it is not as simple as all that. The devotee of the stop-gap God, for example, has something more or less definite to which he can refer with the word God. He cannot see his God, of course, but the *concept* at least is empirical.

The God who meets us in the midst of life, whom we encounter in the limits and demands of existence, cannot be so easily defined. In fact, he cannot be defined at all. He is the undefined, the definition of all that exists. It would be much simpler to call the limit "God's will" and the demand "God's call." But to do so would be to leave us in the context of the stop-gap and escape-hatch God.

The term, "God's will," is helpful in understanding the difficulty twentieth-century man faces in breaking loose from the spiritual context in which he lives. Although it is an ancient term, with a long and honorable tradition, "God's will" emerged in a time when it was yet valid for man to understand his universe as the natural plus the supernatural. But that time is no more. Nothing can bring back a viable supernatural. Occasionally someone suggests that the investigation into ESP (extrasensory perception) is revealing a supernatural reality. The fact is, however, that the investigation is an exploration into as yet not understood phenomena: another instance of the stop-gap God being pushed farther and farther back. Confusion is the most that can be hoped by the use of "God's will" today. At worst—and I suspect most commonly—the demonic power of the stop-gap God is reinforced. For the two words point, for most men, to the supernatural ("God") on the one hand, and the natural ("will") on the other. So we are led into the absurd problem of determining what is "God's will" and what is not, thus setting ourselves in the place of the definer. Dick and Rhonda did not encounter "God's will." They encountered God.

It is almost redundant by this time to say we cannot define the word God. We can no more define the word that points to the reality than we can define God himself. To define anything is to differentiate it from other things, to set limits to its meaning, but God is not a thing, not even a superthing. We cannot define God without playing God in the process. It is not surprising that the ancient Hebrews feared to say the word Yahweh.

For the Hebrews, Yahweh was the one "who brought us out of Egypt," who brought judgment in the form of the Assyrians. Yahweh was met in the events of history. If what happened was for the benefit of the People, it was Yahweh who did it; if for ill to the People, it was Yahweh who did it. They never asked about the character of Yahweh. They only asked about how to respond to what had gone on, was going on, or was to go on in their history.

The same was true of the church that produced the New Testament. In Jesus, called the Christ, men like Paul and the Gospel writers saw an activity they knew as God. Depending on who encountered that activity, it was perceived as good or evil. The disciples said, "You are the Christ, the Son of the Living God." The

Pharisees said, "He casts out demons by the prince of demons."
For the latter, Jesus was anything but God, yet the activity was the
same as it was for the disciples of Jesus.

It is clear from the biblical record, as well as from human experience, that God is a word that points to the character of a man's
relationship to what encounters him in life. It does not point to
an identifiable reality among other realities. God is the name of a
relationship a man has with whatever occurs to him in life. We are
not normally given to naming relationships unless we call them
"good relationships" or "bad relationships" with other people, in
which case we mean we either do or do not get along with another
person. A good relationship is a harmonious one, and a bad relationship is characterized by conflict. But the notion of *naming* the relationship itself seems a bit strange. We can name the other person,
but why name the relationship?

Among primitive peoples, names had magic power; they stood
independent of any reality. The name was, in fact, the reality. The
significance of the often quoted sentence from the second creation
story in Genesis (probably, however, first in order of composition)—
"So out of the ground the LORD God formed every beast of the field
and every bird of the air, and brought them to the man to see what
he would call them; and whatever the man called every living
creature, that was its name"[3]—lies in the power of names. The name
of a person or object was more than the name of the objective
reality—it was the name of the relationship the namer had to it,
a fact of which any parent is well aware. A child is given a name
by his parents in the same way that "the man" named the beasts
and the birds—arbitrarily. But, once given, the name becomes the
way the namer and the named relate to one another. In actuality,
the namer names *both* the named object and his relationship to it.
The name is a symbol that actually is part of the reality which it
signifies. Should the relationship's character change radically, the
name would lose its symbolic nature and become a mere set of
sounds.

The name God, therefore, points both to the absolute limits and
impossible demands that confront a man and to the character of
his relationship with them. The namer—you and I—determines the

name to be given. Today he is called to name the name of God as well as the names of the beasts and birds—and in the naming the reality of God becomes present as genuinely other than the namer. It is not the existence of God as a being that is in question, but the existence of God as a name, a symbol that holds together the entire meaning of life in a single word.

The old Hebrews can help us again. Rather than say Yahweh, God, they said Adononi, Lord. Lord is an identifiable word. A lord is an absolute ruler whose edicts are to be obeyed and who has the power to enforce obedience to them. He is the master of the slave, who owes absolute allegiance to him, who is dependent on him for his very life. Yet Yahweh was not a lord among lords; he was the Lord of lords, the King of kings. These were symbolic and poetic ways of pointing to Yahweh, but they were not Yahweh himself. Yahweh was always the unspeakable, that which was met but never defined.

The Hebrews knew a man could not "see the face of Yahweh and live." To see a face was to understand fully, to become as the one so seen. To "see the face of Yahweh" was to cease being a man: to die. So today we do not see or understand God. We only see, as it were, his backside, as Moses did on the Mountain. We see him as the limit to our existence, as our definition. But we only recognize that limit as God when the limit has become our Lord, with the power of life and death over us.

The fact that this limit has such power is unchanged whether we name it God or the Devil or Fate or anything else. But the name—the symbol—we give it is indicative of the relationship between the final limit and ourselves. While "God" is not simply the name of a relationship, the name is applied only when it points to the final limit and/or absolute demand *and* to the way in which we respond to it. "God" is a genuine symbol. The name participates in the reality toward which it points.

It is absurd to suggest that we should discard the word God, as some would have us do, in favor of another, more "meaningful" term. All so-called synonyms are but euphemisms, not for Yahweh (God) but for Adononi (Lord), which itself merely points to God himself.

Still the question remains unanswered: How can we *possibly* call what says no to our aspirations, and yes to the impossible, God? How is it *possible* to call what encountered me in Dick's death, and what encountered Rhonda in her promotion, God? It is not possible at all—save through "Jesus Christ . . . our Lord, who was conceived by the Holy Ghost, born of the Virgin Mary, suffered under Pontius Pilate, was crucified, dead and buried; he descended into hell; the third day he rose again from the dead; he ascended into heaven, and sitteth at the right hand of God, the Father Almighty; from whence he shall come to judge the quick and the dead."

3

Response to the Limit

dying is fine)but Death

?o
baby
i

wouldn't like
Death if Death
were
good:for

when(instead of stopping to think)you

begin to feel of it,dying
's miraculous
why?be

cause dying is

perfectly natural;perfectly
putting
it mildly lively(but

Death

is strictly
scientific
& artificial &

evil & legal)

we thank thee
god
almighty for dying

(forgive us,o life!the sin of Death

                    e. e. cummings

THE CLOCK in the airport at St. Louis showed late evening. I had about an hour before the flight to Fayetteville, Arkansas, took off—plenty of time to call a friend and chat about old times. The visit was pleasant and ran close to the time for flight departure. I put the phone in its cradle and hurried to the ticket desk to get the gate number for my continuing flight from Washington, D.C.

The clerk took my ticket for the routine check, thumbed through his file, and came up with—nothing. He had no record of the reservation. There would be no problem on that score, he informed me, except the flight was already filled.

But I had made the reservation two weeks before. It had been cleared—it said so right on the ticket. He couldn't help it, he said, there was no record of it in his file, and the flight was filled. He would put me on standby and I could go to the departure gate in the hope someone with confirmed reservations failed to show. I was angry, but I went downstairs and waited.

People came, presented their tickets, and boarded the plane. A whole planeload did so and the aircraft took off. But I didn't. I was stuck in St. Louis—and I had an appointment the next morning that *had* to be kept. I could not possibly stay in St. Louis.

Returning to the ticket desk, I angrily expounded to the innocent clerk that I had to leave *tonight*. He offered some hope. Perhaps in about an hour a plane that had been grounded by mechanical trouble would be able to take off with me, and the others who were waiting, aboard. They had been trying to get it off the ground all day, and he was certain it could leave momentarily.

I went to the airport coffee shop and fumed. An hour passed and I returned to the desk. No plane. The clerk would announce the flight if it were forthcoming. He could assure me, however, that I was confirmed on the early morning flight next day. The hour was late. I had already missed my appointment. I decided there was no sense waiting, and called a hotel.

All the way to the hotel I had to force myself not to inflict my anger upon the cabdriver. Railing at the ticket officer had been fruitless. I could only boil inside—and I did.

Only later did I begin to understand what my response to this highly concrete limit to my desires had been. It was sin.

The Sin Response

The classic definition of sin is "rebellion against God." But today that definition doesn't mean much—if the God rebelled against is the stop-gap and escape-hatch God. To revolt against this God is to deny his existence—the path of traditional atheism. But the existence of God had nothing to do with my difficulty.

There are numbers of things I could have done in the St. Louis airport. I could have waited for the long-delayed—perhaps non-existent—flight. I could have simply slept on a bench until morning. I could have gone—as I did—to a hotel for the night. But certainly I was not about to go into my closet (perhaps a phone booth) and pray God to translate me to my destination or even to bring the promised airplane in the next five minutes. I was, indeed, a *practical* atheist relative to the escape-hatch God. And I'd have been a damn fool otherwise. But the fact that I refused to turn toward the escape-hatch God is no assurance that I was actually serving the God who encountered me at the ticket desk.

I had indeed been in rebellion against God. His no had been clear and inexorable. But I had received it as a purely "immediate" man.[1] I had been met by God himself and had responded by beating my head against him. My head was indeed "bloody but unbowed." The difficulty, of course, is that the situation was unchanged, despite the unbowed, bloody head. I was not finally "master of my fate" or "captain of my soul." Relative to the God of history, failure to acknowledge that fact was sin. I had refused to acknowledge the absolute limit to my own will.

"Rebellion against God" is still a good way of characterizing sin. But when the rebellion is against the definite noes and the impossible demands in life, it looks—and is—radically different from rebellion against the stop-gap and escape-hatch God. At this point rebellion has nothing at all to do with refusal to believe that God (or anything else) exists. It has nothing to do with inability to say creeds or affirm dogmas. Rebellion becomes, rather, specific historical activity in opposition to what limits or demands the impossible. It is an activity that separates a man from himself.

Such was my response to the limitations I met in the St. Louis airport. What had happened simply could not happen. I had to meet my original schedule. It was intolerable that I stay the night in that city. But the truth was, I did not have to proceed; it was not intolerable that I stay. The choice was not between going and not going. That decision had been made—and I did not make it. The choice was: accept the fact and opt for one of the possibilities that fact created, or dissipate my time and energy in railing against it. The choice, in other words, was between faith and sin, between obedience and rebellion. I chose rebellion.

Sin is always an act. It is the implementation of the decision to oppose the divine activity in a man's life. A decision is not always the result of a conscious "decision process." It may be made in a split second without awareness of any consideration of alternatives. Indeed, most decisions are made in this way. I may have trouble deciding to get out of bed in the morning, for example, but I do not even consider the possibility of not tying my shoe laces; nevertheless, I decide daily to do so. As an act, sin is always self-defeating. Men never win in their struggle against God. One might think they would learn that lesson, but they don't. Men continue trying to make the world and their lives into the image of pleasure and harmony they imagine to be perfect.

The world men create for themselves is extremely fragile, a fact amply demonstrated to me by the airline clerk. And, since it is fragile, men spend a great deal of time and energy protecting it, an act that is itself in opposition to God. Their protective mechanism takes the form of anxiety—ambiguous fear—or refusal to trust what they cannot control. Since the world men create for themselves may crack at any moment, they find potential destruction in any thing or person that stands outside their own definition.

Jim, a clergyman of my acquaintance, had spent some years in a serious study of Christian worship. His study had been academic, to be sure, but, in addition, for five years he had gathered with others daily for worship. And he had come to understand the crucial role of communal worship for the life of the church and for the sustenance of the individual.

When he was called by his denomination to become chaplain at a relatively small state university, Jim resolved to assist his students toward a relevant understanding of Christian worship. But he immediately encountered difficulties. The pastor of the church to which the majority of his students flocked on Sunday mornings understood worship in a radically different way. Indeed, Jim was convinced, this man had virtually no consciousness of what worship was all about. Otherwise, why should his morning service be a hodgepodge of irrelevant and misplaced autonomous parts?

Before many months had passed, students began asking Jim about the difference between what he taught and what they saw on Sunday mornings. Jim was pleased, for he saw he had begun to hit the mark. And, although he tried to keep his hostility toward the local pastor out of his conversations with students, they had little difficulty detecting that Jim felt the pastor to be little short of a heretic and to be avoided at all costs.

The struggle between Jim and the pastor began in earnest. They spoke to each other only when necessary for the conduct of general business. Finally, Jim decided the matter had to come to a head. He made an appointment to discuss Christian worship with his ministerial colleague.

They met in the pastor's office. The ensuing conversation, which Jim did not repeat to me in detail, ended in a heated exchange of accusations. Jim accused the pastor of misrepresenting the Christian faith; the pastor accused Jim of taking students away from the church.

In the months that followed, the hostility between the two men intensified and became public knowledge. The root of the trouble was unknown to the college and town community, and finally the two principals themselves were hard pressed to pinpoint the difficulty.

This is a more or less common incident. Most people can tell a similar story from their own experience. In so doing they would be telling the story of their own refusal to trust the other with their own lives. "Life" for both Jim and the pastor was conditioned by the following of college students. An objective observer would have seen values and faults on both sides, but that is beside the point. The genuine issue may only be grasped through a symbol: sin. For Jim and the local pastor, sin became an objective reality—their respective refusal to trust the limit they posed for each other. They had refused to trust the no given to them by the other.

Sin as refusal to trust other people is painful to ourselves and others, but the next logical form of sin is almost unbearable: refusal to trust ourselves, refusal to act on our own decisions.

The schoolboy knows when he is acceptable. His teacher grades his work, allotting it what he considers its merit relative to whatever scale of values under which he may be operating. And the schoolboy knows immediately whether he has done well or has failed or has placed somewhere in between. Even if he has not made top grade, he understands himself to have a place within the system by the very fact the teacher has spent time on his paper and assigned him his place. He knows, too, what he must do to gain greater acceptability from the teacher—and thus in his own eyes.

This same method of receiving assurance of his own trustworthiness is used by the schoolboy as he enters and proceeds through college and, perhaps, graduate school. He is acceptable if the professor says so. But then he is loosed into the world at age twenty-one, twenty-five, or thirty, and there are no teachers anymore, there is no one to say yes or no in unambiguous terms. Value systems are not readily apparent. He has to trust himself.

Having confidence in oneself is not easy, as every man knows. We know we must earn, through demonstrated accomplishment, the right to trust ourselves. But we also know, even the most successful among us, that we are untrustworthy. We know better than anyone else just why we are not to be trusted. And there are times when we hate ourselves for being so weak.

The word for this failure to trust ourselves is sin—the refusal to trust what God has made and declared good. In this world there are no "teachers," no final authorities, no realities to which we may turn for absolute assurance. We are not made "right" by the approval of our spouse, our boss, our friends—but we keep thinking the final authority will appear if we look long enough. It never does; no one wins the race away from God. Sin is self-defeating.

The self-defeat of sin becomes complete when a man begins to distrust everything in general. At this point his very shadow becomes a threat to his self-created world. Only his increasingly narrow sphere appears safe, but, at the same time, he tends to believe the majority of other people are afraid as he is. He and they must protect everyone else against threats from the outside.

These threats are usually given a generic name, such as "communism," under which rubric comes an amazing miscellany of potential dangers. Particularly dangerous are those who do not appear to be afraid of "communism" in the midst. These "unwitting dupes" must be converted to fear in order for everyone to be "safe" and "free."

Often the man possessed by this shadow-fear is religious. He understands God to be on his side, instructing him to protect mankind from the evil one. Indeed, God himself must be protected against the very dangers his worshiper fears, as was demonstrated by the great outcry against the United States Supreme Court decision that state-ordered prayers and Bible-reading in the public schools are unconstitutional.

The sketch above admittedly is a caricature, but it comes closer to reality than most of us like to think, particularly the man so possessed. He has gone full circle in rebellion against God, who receives all of life, including what men fear and what men love. Paul's words to the Romans come as a great affront if they are seen as relevant at all: "For none of us lives for himself only, none of us dies for himself only; if we live, it is for the Lord that we live, and if we die, it is for the Lord that we die. Whether we live or die, then, we belong to the Lord."[2]

Once more it must be recognized that, even for the man of shadow-fear, sin is an act, a decision, a response to the God who meets him in the midst of life. A man need not be religious to sin, for the God who meets him in the limits and impossible demands of life meets all men alike; God is known to every man from birth. Paul began his letter to the Romans with that fact in mind:

God's wrath is revealed coming down from heaven upon all the sin and evil of men, whose evil ways prevent the truth from being known. God punishes them, because what men can know about God is plain to them. God himself made it plain to them. Ever since God created the world, his invisible qualities, both his eternal power and his divine nature, have been clearly seen. Men can perceive them in the things that God has made. So they have no excuse at all! They know God, but they do not give him the glory that belongs to him, nor do they thank him. Instead, their thoughts have become complete nonsense and their empty minds are filled with darkness. They say they are wise, but they are fools; they exchange the glory of the immortal God for images made to look like mortal man, birds, animals, and reptiles.

Because men are such fools, God has given them over to do the filthy things their hearts desire, and they do shameful things with each other. They exchange the truth about God for a lie; they worship and serve what God has created instead of the Creator himself, who is to be praised forever! Amen.[3]

Paul clearly did not suggest that God is to be worshiped as "nature." But his positive declaration is equally clear: God encounters all men "in the things he has made," none of which are God in themselves. God is always present, demanding a choice between acknowledgment of his "eternal power" or rebellion against him by exchanging "the glory of the immortal God for images made to look like mortal man, etc." The consequence (which is commonly, but mistakenly, called sin) of this rebellion is that men do "shameful things with each other"—the reduplication of unacknowledged defeat.

The biblical understanding of sin is a wrong choice, a wrong action, a decisive act of distrust in God.[4] The history of the Christian community through the centuries confirms the rebellious character of sin. Every time the church, and its individual personifications (members), "comes to itself," it confesses its decision to reject God as God. So the Prayer of General Confession reads: "Almighty and most merciful Father; we have erred, and strayed from thy ways like lost sheep. We have followed too much the devices and desires of our own hearts. We have offended against thy holy laws. We have left undone those things which we ought to have done; and we have done those things which we ought not to have done; and there is no health in us. But thou, O Lord, have mercy upon us, miserable offenders."

It is not necessary, however, to turn to the liturgy or church history to understand ourselves as sinful actors. All we need is to
become conscious of living before the God of history. All we need,
in other words, is to become human beings—men.

As we have seen, we are quite adept at dodging the demand
placed upon us to be men. One of the ways commonly used is to
equate sin with "naughtiness" (the consequences of sin). Men then
assume they may become righteous by altering a particular form of
conduct and remain so by abstinence from it. Righteousness or non-
sin may be secured by obedience to the law, a "created thing."
Clearly, such righteousness is sin itself, and a most insidious form
at that, for it places God's sanction on the rebellious decision to
worship and serve the creature (law) rather than the Creator.

In whatever form it takes, sin is an act men perform almost constantly. For this reason, sin is sometimes considered a state. Man,
according to this view, is sinful by nature, and Christian theology
has offered the myth of the Fall as evidence of this all-pervasive
character of humankind. But there is a difference between an un-
changing state and an observation that men consistently elect for
rebellion against God.

A careful reading of the Genesis account of the Fall reveals
that the man and the woman had a genuine choice between obedience to the command of God or rebellion against it. They chose
rebellion. But they did not have to do so! Once a man comes to
understand that this myth is not an account of something that happened a very long time ago, conditioning all subsequent human existence, he is free to see it as a marvelous mirror reflecting the
existential choice presented to every man at each juncture of daily
life. Everyone must constantly decide between sin and faith, between distrust and trust. And men are wondrously blessed in that
the alternative to sin is presented to them in an unambiguous
symbolic form: Jesus Christ.

The Christ Response

Unlike the divine activity in life, the Christ response to that
activity is not immediately apparent to every man. It may properly

be said that the response of Jesus Christ is alien to man. It is impossible. A man would never think of it himself. But it is impossible only so long as a man insists on life being shaped in his own image. The simplicity—and the genuine difficulty—of the Christ response becomes evident only after its acceptance.

What is the Christ response to God, the absolute limit and impossible demand? Negatively, it is the direct opposite of the sin response. In Christ, a man refuses to receive the events of his life —the pleasurable ones, the painful ones, and the daily ones—as threats to his significance. Positively, the Christ response is the hard, indeed painful decision to trust the significance of oneself to the very absolute limits and impossible demands that threaten one's sinful self. The Christ response to life lies in receiving everything that comes as one receives any great, good gift. In Christ, all the events that comprise a man's existence are joyfully entered, for they are *very good.*

Augustine, speaking existentially in an essential context, wrote: "And aught else besides Thee was there not, whereof Thou mightest create them, O God, One Trinity, and Triune Unity; and therefore out of nothing didst Thou create heaven and earth; a great thing, and a small thing; for Thou art Almighty and Good, to make all things good, even the great heaven, and the petty earth."[5] Countless times I have witnessed men and women "come apart at the seams" at the fourth-century theologian's radical affirmation. "All things are *not* good—look at the suffering in the world!" Just so. From the vantage point of the stop-gap and escape-hatch God, there are indeed goods and bads in the world. Men all operate on this assumption. A radical reunderstanding of the word good is required, and that new understanding bears the symbolic name Christ.

In common practice a man receives a given occurrence as bad or good depending on whether or not it is in harmony with his standard or hope. These words are symbols for men's response to the occurrence, a response that depends on the value system upon which they, usually unconsciously, operate. But what if the standard were different?

The Christ response to divine activity is founded on a unique value standard. Whereas the usual standard is a man's own pleasure (projected to a general norm), the Christ response is based on what God does. Further, it assumes that nothing transpires apart from God. In the Christ response, a man simply acquiesces in a judgment already made—all that is is good. The explicit biblical testimony to the goodness of all things, and the fact that goodness is a value judgment, is found, of course, in Genesis 1, in which God declares his creation to be very good.

Such acquiescence does not come naturally. Men live the majority of their lives as "immediate" men, responding as bugs to anything that happens. They are enabled to make the Christ response only when it has been presented to them as a genuine possibility—which bears the name Jesus Christ.

Through the centuries, Christians have spoken of the Christ in their lives as a sudden and cataclysmic event. It is something out of the ordinary. They have told of it as a miracle, a wonder—for such it is. But the marvelous character of Christ's advent has often been perverted into a mechanism for salvation by the stop-gap and escape-hatch God. One may know Christ has come when he feels his presence. Thus, ways have been devised to create the presence of Christ.

Yet, Christ as the saving possibility is not, first of all, an emotion or psychological occurrence. It is the concrete availability of a real alternative response to what comes in life. It does not twist his arm to make a man choose its way; it is just there. Such was the way Christ came to Paul on the road to Damascus. He told it as a genuine marvel. An examination of his speech before King Agrippa will be instructive for twentieth-century man's encounter with the same event.

> I myself thought that I should do everything I could against the name of Jesus of Nazareth. That is what I did in Jerusalem. I received authority from the chief priests and put many of God's people in prison; and when they were sentenced to death, I voted against them. Many times I had them punished in all the Jewish meeting houses, and tried to make them deny their faith. I was so furious with them that I even went to foreign cities to persecute them.
>
> It was for this purpose that I went to Damascus with the authority and orders from the chief priests. It was on the road at midday, your Majesty,

that I saw a light much brighter than the sun shining from the sky around me and the men traveling with me. All of us fell to the ground, and I heard a voice say to me in the Hebrew language, 'Saul, Saul! Why are you persecuting me? You hurt yourself by hitting back, like an ox kicking against its owner's stick.' 'Who are you, Lord?' I asked. And the Lord said: 'I am Jesus, whom you persecute. But get up and stand on your feet. I have appeared to you to appoint you as my servant; you are to tell others what you have seen of me today, and what I will show you in the future. I will save you from the people of Israel and from the Gentiles, to whom I will send you. You are to open their eyes and turn them from the darkness to the light, and from the power of Satan to God, so that through their faith in me they will have their sins forgiven and receive their place among God's chosen people.'

And so, King Agrippa, I did not disobey the vision I had from heaven.[6]

Paul's history is not dissimilar to contemporary men's. As he, they have spent their time and energy in obedience (or rebellion—inverted obedience) to the law. They have been certain that their own understanding of life, including religion, was the only true way. They have been impatient with those who disagreed, if they have not actually persecuted them. Indeed, they would have been foolish otherwise.

More common, however, is man's history of constant opposition to the possibility of life's goodness in such events as I experienced in the St. Louis airport. I had known of the Christ possibility; indeed, I had studied it and believed I lived by it. But when the chips were down, I rejected it. No light from the sky fell upon me at the airline ticket desk. That happened later.

It happened as I was recounting the episode to a friend two days after—still angry. It happened when he said, "Oh, come on! You're just hurting yourself fighting it." In a flash, the question came to me: "Saul, Saul! Why are you persecuting me? You hurt yourself by hitting back, like an ox kicking against its owner's stick." Of course. Banging my head against God and the possibility offered in Christ only got my head bloody. It was *hard* kicking against the stick.

The stick, of course, is the presence of the absolute negations and the impossible demands meeting all men in the everyday happenings of life. Paul was saying that distrust of the God he encountered in Jesus was defeat itself. But he was also saying that the alternative was present in the very awareness of self-defeat. It was no longer necessary to fight against what the King James Version calls the "pricks." The battle was over.

Is it possible to trust our lives into the hands of God? The witness of the New Testament is an emphatic yes. If the doctrine of the Incarnation means anything today, it means that we have the living historical testament to the possibility of trusting God with our whole beings. In Jesus we have the prototype of the faithful man, the man who moves through life in the secure confidence that his existence and its significance is not dependent on what he does or who he is. In Jesus we have the picture of a man who lives the possibility of trusting God to take care of him, as the flowers of the field so trust. Jesus "pronounces woes on his betrayer, yet the son of man goes as it has been determined, not by betrayer but by the will beyond all finite wills."[7]

Jesus Christ represents the concrete historical possibility of living with childlike (not childish!) trust in what comes over life's hill, trust in God. But simply because one man so lived does not diminish the difficulty of trusting ("faithing") God today. And the life of Jesus certainly lays no obligation on us to trust. The life affirmation offered in Jesus Christ involves what we all know as death—the abandonment of all our previous allegiances to moral standards, parental images, institutional edicts; abandonment, in other words, of all to which we have clung for life's significance, and placing every last bit of trust in God. "Where there is faith in God as the ultimate reality," Bonhoeffer wrote, "all concern with ethics will have as its starting point that God shows Himself to be good, even if this involves the risk that myself and the world are not good but thoroughly bad."[8]

The possibility offered in Jesus Christ is the real possibility of receiving all that is as good.[9] It is the possibility of living the new creation, existence before the Fall. The second Genesis story tells us that men are alienated from God because they insist on knowing both good *and* evil. They insist, that is, on being able to determine what should and should not exist (for only the good has the right to exist; evil, by definition, ought not to be). "To know good and evil is to know oneself as the origin of good and evil, as the origin of an eternal choice and election."[10] And that is exactly what the Christian faith knows as sin.

Both sin and the possibility offered in Jesus Christ are available for our choosing in the mid-twentieth century. While freely acknowledging that, along with Christian men through history, they constantly choose sin, men still have the option of consciously choosing Christ as the operating mode or Lord of their existence.

There should be no surprise that the possibility does not occur as a matter of course. It is literally an absurd statement, an absurd possibility. Every man knows his life depends on the approval of his boss, the love of his wife, the assurance of an income. Without these—or others any given person could list—life would fall apart. Men cling to their created deities (they don't call them God—if they did they would, like Faust, enter into conscious rebellion against the God of history, something found only in literature) with demonic tenacity. Thus, the possibility in Jesus Christ must be offered from outside. Praise God, it is!

John, a Gospel writer who self-consciously related the Christ possibility to men of his day in narrative style, offers numerous didactic anecdotes pointing to the possibility of new life. One of the justly famous of these is found in his Chapter 9:

> As Jesus walked along he saw a man who had been born blind. His disciples asked him: "Teacher, whose sin was it that caused him to be born blind? His own or his parents' sin?" Jesus answered: "His blindness has nothing to do with his sins or his parents' sins. He is blind so that God's power might be seen at work in him. We must keep on doing the works of him who sent me so long as it is day; the night is coming, when no one can work. While I am in the world I am the light for the world." After he said this, Jesus spat on the ground and made some mud with the spittle; he put the mud on the man's eyes, and told him, "Go wash your face in the Pool of Siloam." (This name means "Sent.") So the man went, washed his face, and came back seeing.
>
> His neighbors, then, and the people who had seen him begging before this, asked, "Isn't this the man who used to sit and beg?" Some said, "He is the one," but others said, "No, he is not, he just looks like him." So the man himself said, "I am the man." "How were your eyes opened?" they asked him. He answered, "The man named Jesus made some mud, put it on my eyes, and told me, 'Go to Siloam and wash your face.' So I went, and as

soon as I washed I could see." "Where is he?" they asked. "I do not know,"
he answered.

Then they took the man who had been blind to the Pharisees. The day that
Jesus made the mud and opened the man's eyes was a Sabbath. The Pharisees, then, asked the man again how he had received his sight. He told them,
"He put some mud on my eyes, I washed my face, and now I can see." Some
of the Pharisees said, "The man who did this cannot be from God because
he does not obey the Sabbath law." Others, however, said, "How could a
man who is a sinner do such mighty works as these?" And there was a division among them.

So the Pharisees asked the man once more, "You say he opened your eyes—
well, what do you say about him?" "He is a prophet," he answered. The
Jews, however, were not willing to believe that he had been blind and could
now see, until they called the man's parents and asked them: "Is this your
son? Do you say that he was born blind? Well, how is it that he can see
now?" His parents answered: "We know that he is our son, and we know
that he was born blind. But we do not know how it is that he is now able
to see, nor do we know who opened his eyes. Ask him; he is old enough,
and he can answer for himself!" His parents said this because they were
afraid of the Jews; for the Jews had already agreed that if anyone confessed
that Jesus was the Messiah he would be put out of the meeting house. That
is why his parents said, "He is old enough; ask him!"

A second time they called back the man who had been born blind and said
to him, "Promise before God that you will tell the truth! We know that this
man is a sinner." "I do not know if he is a sinner or not," the man replied.
"One thing I do know: I was blind, and now I see." "What did he do to
you?" they asked. "How did he open your eyes?" "I have already told you,"
he answered, "and you would not listen. Why do you want to hear it again?
Maybe you, too, would like to be his disciples?" They cursed him and said:
"You are that fellow's disciple: we are Moses' disciples. We know that God
spoke to Moses: as for that fellow, we do not even know where he comes
from!" The man answered: "What a strange thing this is! You do not know
where he comes from, but he opened my eyes! We know that God does not
listen to sinners; he does listen to people who respect him and do what he
wants them to do. Since the beginning of the world it has never been heard
of that someone opened the eyes of a blind man; unless this man came from
God, he would not be able to do a thing." They answered back, "You were
born and raised in sin—and you are trying to teach us?" And they threw
him out of the meeting house.

Jesus heard that they had thrown him out. He found him and said, "Do
you believe in the Son of Man?" The man answered, "Tell me who he is,

sir, so I can believe in him!" Jesus said to him, "You have already seen him, and he is the one who is talking with you now." "I believe, Lord!" the man said, and knelt down before Jesus.

Jesus said, "I came to this world to judge, so that the blind should see, and those who see should become blind." Some Pharisees, who were there with him, heard him say this and asked him, "You don't mean that we are blind, too?" Jesus answered, "If you were blind, then you would not be guilty; but since you say, 'We can see,' that means that you are still guilty."[11]

The disciples raised a question that sounds quite modern. They wanted to know the *reason* for the suffering before them. The question sounds almost scientific: if the causes could be determined, guilt could be assessed, responsibility placed, and the problem dismissed. Jesus' answer has been disturbing to generations of Christians (does he mean to say God made the man blind?). It was an answer that cut through all rational and scientific issues, straight to the existential question: "Here is a blind man, let's not worry about cause and effect. He is blind in the present, not in the past. You want a cause? God is the cause. But we've got a job to do, a Word to declare, let's get on with it." So he put some mud on the man's face and told him to wash it off.

Jesus, it should be noted, made no promises to the man. He merely told him to wash his face. It was something anyone would do if someone came and smeared mud on him. The blind man didn't face any great decision. But, as John tells it, the blind man isn't really the point ("He is blind so that God's power might be seen at work in him"). The point is that when Christ appears, new life is present, new ways of seeing reality become conscious. Such was indeed the case—the man could see and so could the neighbors.

To the neighbors, the formerly blind man was both the same and different. He appeared to be the blind man—but he could see. The man gave his own answer: "I am the man." He was indeed the same man, but everything was different. The difference was Christ, a radically new life—for the same man.

When asked about his new sight, the man made no attempt at interpretation. He simply cited the sequence of events. He made no judgment on the one who had smeared his face. He didn't even know where he had gone. After all, how irrelevant can you get? His new sight was what mattered. Did it really make any difference that *Jesus* had put the paste on him? He had met the Christ, the new possibility, and he himself was living testimony to it. He had no formula for duplication of his recovery. There is, of course, no such formula. Either one has heard the possibility in Christ and accepted it (washed the mud from his eyes), or one hasn't.

The established order immediately got in on the act. To its representatives the issue wasn't that a man had been ushered into new life. The question was: Had a rule been violated? In investigating violation of the law, the Pharisees followed what would be considered good practice today. They checked on the facts. Was the man actually born blind? Yes. Had he actually received his sight? Yes. What do you think about it? The prosecuting attorney on a Perry Mason show couldn't have put the answer given by the parents better: it was a question calling for a conclusion. The parents, however, were not arguing a legal point. They were scared, and didn't want to get involved. Besides, the point of the story is not the response of the parents, but what happens when a man runs into Jesus Christ.

Thus, the Pharisees turned to the man himself. They had already heard the story from him once, but that wasn't sufficient. He had only evaluated Jesus as a prophet. Anyone could be a prophet, prophets were all over the place. And prophets don't change a man's life in such a radical way. So they pressed him, putting the issue in terms of whether Jesus was a sinner or not. We have seen that a sinner is one who rebels against the reality that is God. But the Pharisees' definition was different: a sinner violated the law.

It was an irrelevant context to the man born blind. It is an irrelevant context to modern men, who are also born blind to the possibility offered in the encounter with Christ. The man couldn't have cared less. He used to be blind; now he could see. What more was needed? What relevance does the violation of some law have to that? Who Jesus was, his authority, his status, was an irrelevant question. What was significant was what he did. And it was unimportant even to inquire where he came from.

But the question of Jesus' origin was important for the Pharisees. The Messiah was supposed to come from Bethlehem, a fact that

Matthew and Luke were careful to establish. This fellow had an unknown origin. No sign had appeared that they could see. The born-blind man was completely unconcerned. All he knew was he could see—that was enough. But what more sign did they need than this newly acquired sight?

Twentieth-century men are not interested in labels either. They are pragmatic beings. What are the results? It makes no difference what you call him, does he actually bring off what is claimed of him? The Pharisees established that fact; they just didn't like what it meant relative to their scale of values. There was simply no room in their system for such a radical change in response to life.

The word of a new possible response to life, the word of new life itself, comes to men today in ways they cannot identify. But they don't care, so long as it comes. The new way of relating to life is more significant than the opinion of those in authority. It is more important than being admitted to the synagogue. The new man is free, even from the highest temporal authority. He is free. Period. The freshly sighted man used to sit and beg, dependent subserviently on the handouts of others. But later he was able to talk back to the eminent Pharisees. He was his own man. The past was past. "The old has passed away; behold the new has come."

A man's freedom, his "Christ-dom," is not dependent upon a particular formulation of doctrine. It is not even dependent on the word Christ. The cured man had to be told—later—the identity of the one who had healed him. Only then was he able to *worship* the "Son of Man."

The man who responds to life in Jesus Christ says no to the past. He doesn't, of course, ignore the events of past history. He knows he can never be other than the one who has lived the life he has lived, in the culture in which he has lived, with its history. But he rejects completely his past way of relating to the God who meets him in history. He rejects his refusal to trust others, himself, and everything-in-general. He turns around, as it were, to go in the opposite direction. And this is what the New Testament means by *metanoia*, repentance.

What does it mean to trust oneself, others, and everything-in-general? What does it mean to trust God? It does not mean that one

goes through life naïvely believing what any and everyone says
or does. Far from it. The man who responds to life in Jesus Christ
sees, more clearly than anyone else, the actual significance of events
about him. Sensitive as he is to the ever present danger of obedience
to created things, he knows when this obedience is expressed by
those about him. He is aware, usually later (as was my case relative
to the airline), of sin as his own response to God. He knows that,
as he himself is untrustworthy, others are as well. The man who
responds to life in Jesus Christ does not accept the world at face
value.

Just because the Christ-man does not accept men and events at
face value, but understands the *actual* ways they respond to divine
activity, he is able to accept them for what they are, without necessity of protecting himself against them. The self he doesn't protect,
of course, is his own face value. His life significance is utterly secure,
for he knows that whether he lives or dies, he is the Lord's. Before
the final noes and impossible demands he knows himself to be good.

No man can receive the wonderful possibility offered in Jesus
Christ without becoming a new man. And as such, a tremendously
heavy burden is placed upon him. But it is a burden he finds light
nevertheless. It is a burden he carries as offhandedly as a strong man
bears a little boy. What is the burden? Paul suggested it when he
testified before King Agrippa that he "did not disobey the heavenly
vision."

Who would not find it a burden to change his entire life-style?
Yet that is what Paul did. In so doing he let the future determine
his present. As the zealous Pharisee he had been threatened at the
challenge to the solidified past presented by the followers of Jesus.
He had worked tooth and claw to shape the present in the image of
the past. As a Christ-man, he was able and willing to take whatever
the future brought as the context of God's world, calling him to
declare the Christ possibility in it.

The sinful response to life always finds the changing present to
be a threat, because it always comes as something new and different
from the familiar ways. The Christ response, on the other hand,
looks to the future, is open to the future, to what will happen. In
St. Louis my attention was wholly directed toward what should

have been, what I had planned, what had taken place to bring the situation I faced in the moment. I was concerned to change the past, or, rather, to change the future so that the past would be as though it hadn't been. The trouble was, the past wouldn't change. Try as I might, I could do nothing to alter what was. Acting in rebellion against God, I tried to find out what had caused the reservation problem as though that would make it go away. But even had I chased it down, the clerk assured me, the plane would still have been filled.

In Christ, on the other hand, attention is directed to the future, accepting the past (including the present) as a given. The Christ response asks what possibilities are now opened up, where can we go from here. It affirms what has happened as good at the very time it may be unhappy about it. In Christ, the future conditions the present; in sin, the past is sole determinant.

In sum, therefore, the possible response to God offered in Christ opens the whole future for fearless creative activity; the absolute limits and impossible claims become great opportunities to move into the uncharted unknown. Does the Christ-man fear? His emotions fear, his mind fears—but his self moves nevertheless.

Even though the Christ possibility be offered, it need not be accepted. A man may elect to remain in his sin. Paul's account of his encounter on the road to Damascus and John's story of the man born blind may sound as though acceptance were automatic. It simply doesn't happen that way apart from literature (of which the New Testament is a part). How is acceptance of this absurd possibility possible?

It is not—unless one believes in the Holy Ghost.

4

The Decisive Spirit

SONG OF A MAN WHO HAS COME THROUGH

Not I, not I, but the wind that blows through me!
A fine wind is blowing the new direction of Time.
If only I let it bear me, carry me, if only it carry me!
If only I am sensitive, subtle, oh, delicate, a winged gift!
If only, most lovely of all, I yield myself and am borrowed
By the fine, fine wind that takes its course through the chaos of the world
Like a fine, an exquisite chisel, a wedge-blade inserted;
If only I am keen and hard like the sheer tip of a wedge
Driven by invisible blows,
The rock will split, we shall come at the wonder, we shall find the
 Hesperides.

Oh, for the wonder that bubbles into my soul,
I would be a good fountain, a good well-head,
Would blur no whisper, spoil no expression.

What is the knocking?
What is the knocking at the door in the night?
It is somebody wants to do us harm.

No, no, it is the three strange angels.
Admit them, admit them.

D. H. LAWRENCE

I FIRST MET Janice and Henry Simon at the home of a mutual friend. The party was congenial all around, but I was impressed by the vivacity displayed by the Simons. No one had a better time and no one seemed to have better prospects.

Henry had just taken a new job that entailed a substantially greater amount of responsibility than anything he had done before—and he was discovering himself quite capable of handling it. Janice had begun to experience the exhilarating freedom that came with her fourth child growing out of diapers. The future brightened their present.

Immediately attracted to the Simons, my wife and I cultivated their friendship. During the course of the following months, as the friendship matured, we discovered that behind the free gaiety evident at the party lay the immediate necessity to make a major decision, a decision that presented no pleasant alternative at all.

The Simons were hopelessly in debt. Not the kind of debt that requires temporary tightening of the belt, but a matter of at least two years' salary—with the legal requirement to pay it off within three years. Somehow, they had been managing to make the payments, although the constant pressure on family and personal life from lack of sufficient funds for daily necessities was beginning to take its toll. At that point, Janice became pregnant. It was the final straw.

Henry and Janice examined their situation thoroughly, desperately searching for something that would allow them to avoid the personal bankruptcy that seemed inevitable. Nothing presented itself, except the possibility of giving up their home (rented) and moving into a barn at the home of Janice's parents, who lived in a suburb some sixty miles from Henry's office. It hardly seemed a solution to the Simons, even though they would then have been able to apply substantially all their rent money toward debt retirement. The barn could be made livable, granted. But Henry would have to take a room in the city (their ancient auto was not up to the daily 120-mile trip) and would be able to join the family only on weekends. But, worst of all, the move would require reopening of parental conflicts that had long lain dormant. All in all, the prospect of moving seemed quite on a par with bankruptcy proceedings in its anguish quotient. Nevertheless, a decision had to be made—and no ready-made rules would serve to make it for them.

One morning, so they told us later, Janice looked at Henry and simply said, "Let's move out of here." Henry looked back and said, "I'll rent a trailer this weekend." And so he did. The decision had been made.

Several weeks later, my wife and I visited the Simons at their new barn—and found new people. "The weeks that preceded our decision to move here were hell," Janice told us. "We both nearly fell apart. We felt as if moving here would be unbearable. But once we *acted* on our decision, we suddenly felt damned good. It's something we can't explain. We don't know what the consequences will be, but somehow that's okay."

Listening to her talk, I suddenly began to understand what was happening before my very eyes. I was witnessing the Holy Spirit.

The Impossible Decision

There is scarcely a symbol in the Christian tradition that has been more neglected, ignored, misunderstood, exalted, and extolled than the Holy Spirit. The Apostles' Creed details what is suggested by "God" and goes on at length about Jesus Christ—but simply mentions the Holy Spirit. On the other hand, spiritualist sects through the centuries have hinged their doctrine and practice on "receiving the Spirit." There is validity in each approach.

In the approach that seems to neglect the Holy Spirit is the wisdom that before the decision to receive the Christ response to life, the Spiritual symbol is worse than meaningless. At that time, nothing is to be gained by hearing about the divine Spirit. The Holy Spirit cannot be appropriated; it can only be received and acknowledged. It cannot be bought or borrowed but comes as a completely free gift, over which the recipient—or nonrecipient—has no control. The framers of the Creed were right in assuming those who were to repeat it would need no explication of the Holy Spirit. They would know the Holy Spirit to be the symbol operative in the declaration of the Creed.

The so-called spiritualist groups recognize and emphasize the magnificence and wonder of the gift that is the Holy Spirit. But it is not surprising that, as they become older and institutionally solidified, the emphasis tends to change. Revelry in the Holy Spirit, intense as it may be, is brief; then those who have received it settle down to a fervent declaration of the Christ. Nevertheless, the Pentecostal groups have their finger on the truth that the Holy Spirit is the symbolic necessity for saying Christ and God.

When the Christ possibility is presented, it comes as impossible, certainly as offering no solution to whatever situation in which one finds oneself. It does not offer, in other words, what each of us wants—an escape hatch, something to make the problem go away, producing peace of mind. Certainly no escape hatch was offered to Janice and Henry, by Christ or anyone else. Confronted by God in the absolute barrier to life as they wished it in their financial dilemma, they chose not to decide. For weeks after Janice's pregnancy was known they refused to make a decision about their future. But not making a decision was a decision nevertheless, the decision of sin, as we have seen. It was the decision, as Janice told me, to live in hell. Her term was exactly correct: hell is the life of those who refuse to come to terms with the absolute limits and impossible demands, who refuse to come to terms with God.

Janice and Henry were not alone in their hell, however, for, in their encounter with God, life-possibilities opened for them that were not present before: bankruptcy and moving to a parents' barn. In these possibilities came the demand we have already come to know as God, and in that demand was the possibility of free life we have seen in Christ. But the Christ possibility that entered the Simons' lives did not promise anything they wanted; rather, it forced them to deal seriously with their lives, something few of us ever want to do. The possibility of life in Jesus Christ is still a "stumbling block to the Jews and folly to the Greeks."

It is a stumbling block because it is a life orientation that cannot be secured by a prearranged process. The "Jew" in each of us demands a rule, by obedience to which we may secure what we desire, whether we call it happiness, the Kingdom of God, eternal salvation, or prosperity. But Christ does not offer such an easy solution to the knotty issues we face. He simply offers a *possible* response to them—and declares it to be the only life-giving response available.

That possible response is equally folly, for the "Greek" in us wants to know the eternal verities of life. We want to be initiated into the mysteries of life and death, which, once known, will make all subsequent decisions automatic. But Christ does not offer absolute knowledge and eternal security. He only presents a possible response to whatever happens in life—and shoves us even farther into involvement with the life we want to avoid.

It doesn't help much to tell the man confronted with this impossible possibility that the Holy Spirit will help him make his decision. If he has been trained as a religious man, such a declaration only increases his sense of frustration at not feeling the Spirit nearby, thus adding another barrier between him and his potential humanity. If he has little emotional identification with Christian doctrine, he will consider the mention of the Holy Spirit foolish piety, again raising a barrier between him and genuine freedom.

The Holy Spirit is not an evangelistic symbol. It is a symbol within the lives of the Saints. There it has the most profound meaning, for those who have chosen to receive the possibility offered in Jesus Christ know they could never accept it as their life response apart from the agency of the Holy Spirit. They know that the impossible decision—which they had to make as absolutely lonely individuals— could not possibly have been made without the active gift of life in the Christ response to the demand of God, which was translated into the symbol, Holy Spirit, in their affirmative answer. My life is entirely my own responsibility. Period. My life is entirely the gift of God. Period. Both statements are absolutely true.

We may have little difficulty understanding what is meant by the first part of the paradox (if not in receiving it!), but what could it possibly mean to say that God, the encounter with absolute limits and impossible demands, *gives* me my life? Serious consideration of the question is crucial to a contemporary understanding of the Holy Spirit.

No gift is a gift unless it is received. Everyone has had the experience of being given things he did not want to accept for one reason or another. A gift that is forced on a person is no gift at all, but a bondage of which the gift is sign and symbol.

I once chose to give a Christmas present to a friend, and, in order to make certain he would receive it on Christmas morning, placed it without his knowledge among other packages under the decorated tree in his home. In the rush of seasonal activities, I forgot about the small box—until late Christmas day, when my friend appeared at my door. Hastily, he had located a present, wrapped it up, and was delivering it to me in person. This man chose not to receive my gift; he chose to purchase it, thus negating the gift character of my present.

This episode serves to illustrate the two major prerequisites for any gift: it must be freely given and it must be freely received. When a gift is given in such a way that the recipient knows something is expected of him in return, the gift is not a gift. Conversely, a gift that is received with a sense of reciprocal obligation is not received as a gift but as a purchase for which payment is due. A genuine gift places no obligation on either the giver or the recipient. Gifts are free. Life is not exempt from the conditions that constitute any other gift. If I am to be given my life, I must receive my life. And I must receive it as a gift. That is, I must receive it as provided—without conditions.

Life always comes to us in terms of limitation and demand, in which context the possibility of receiving it just as it comes is offered in Jesus Christ. We are not called on to pay anything for our life. It is ours for the taking—but it must be taken. Thus it is possible to say symbolically, "God gives me my life"—and thereby point to the unconditional character of our human existence—and it is equally possible to say that I receive my life as a gift, through the agency of the Holy Spirit.

The story of the events at Pentecost following the death of Jesus is of assistance in revealing the Holy Spirit as the decision to receive the Christ response to life:

> When the day of Pentecost arrived, all the believers were gathered together in one place. Suddenly there was a noise from the sky which sounded like a

strong wind blowing, and it filled the whole house where they were sitting. Then they saw what looked like tongues of fire spreading out; and each person there was touched by a tongue. They were all filled with the Holy Spirit and began to talk in other languages, as the Spirit enabled them to speak.[1]

The apostles had never understood what Jesus had been telling them while he was alive.[2] They continually wanted to put him into their own context. Even in Acts, before the Pentecost account, they had wanted to know, "Lord, is this the time when you are to *establish once again the sovereignty of Israel?*"[3]

Throughout the synoptic Gospels, Jesus is reported as going about making it clear that men may be free from bondage to whatever binds them. But the disciples, unlike the demons and healed persons, never seemed to understand that simple and observable fact. They followed Jesus because they thought he held a hope for the future, a hope for the reestablishment of the sovereignty of Israel. But when he told a story or pulled off a healing, they wanted to know the meaning. John finally summed up the matter in his Gospel: "For a long time I have been with you all; yet you do not know me, Philip? Whoever has seen me has seen the Father. Why, then, do you say, 'Show us the Father'?"[4]

When Jesus was killed, the disciples' hope died too. Huddling together in fear of the present consequences of trailing after the convicted revolutionary, they kept their number intact after the defection of Judas, but they lacked the courage to *be* the resurrected Christ—until the Spirit came or, as we might say today, they decided to receive the Word they had been hearing all along. What, then, is the Pentecost story all about? It's about the Holy Spirit. But it really doesn't tell us very much about the divine Spirit; it tells us a great deal more about what happens to men who decide to receive the Christ possibility.

We should not be surprised that Luke doesn't tell us much directly about the Holy Spirit. As we have seen, there is precious little we may know about God or Christ either. God is known as definition. Christ is known as possibility. And now the Holy Spirit is seen to be decision, a man's own decision to receive the Christ possibility, the only life-giving possibility available.

The disciples began to "talk in other tongues." They became eloquent and convincing about the Word embodied in Jesus the Christ. Everybody could understand clearly the possibility being offered to him. Some people wanted to know the significance for themselves of what they saw and heard. Others made a judgment: "They have been drinking." It was a natural response. Some years ago a popular song appeared that declared the desire of a lover to "wake the town and tell the people" of his love for the loved one. Should he have done so, he would have met a response like that the disciples did: "He must be drunk!"

Peter then took it upon himself to make a speech. No, they were not drunk. They had simply decided to receive the Word of Christ that had been present with them all along in Jesus. And what a Word it was! They were ecstatic in glee—it was the most wonderful possibility ever, and everyone must know of it. The disciples' action and Peter's sermon *were* the Holy Spirit.

But Peter did not preach about the Holy Spirit. He preached about Jesus Christ, for Christ was the objective referent of his and the other apostles' ecstasy. The listeners were to respond toward Jesus Christ, not the Holy Spirit. The listeners were not called on to respond toward someone else's decision: they were called on to make their own decision about the Christ possibility. When Peter's hearers, "deeply troubled," wanted to know, "What shall we do, brothers?", Peter said to them: "Turn away from your sins, each one of you, and be baptized in the name of Jesus Christ, so that your sins will be forgiven; and you will receive God's gift, the Holy Spirit."[5]

It should be clear by now that repentance means an active decision to turn one's back on self-defeating modes of relating to God in the everyday situations of life. And it should be clear that repentance entails, positively, acceptance of the possibility offered in Jesus Christ. The disciples had decided to make the Christ Word the operating mode (Lord) of their lives. And that decision is the activity known symbolically as the Holy Spirit.

Another New Testament passage demonstrates that not every encounter with the Christ possibility is an occasion for the Holy Spirit. The account of Jesus' meeting with the rich young man has been a puzzle to men ever since it was written down, if not before. How could the young man dare reject Christ? Mark's version of the story is addressed to the question:

> As Jesus was starting again on his trip, a man ran up, knelt before him, and asked him: "Good Teacher, what must I do to receive eternal life?" "Why do you call me good?" Jesus asked him. "No one is good except God alone. You know the commandments: 'Do not murder; do not commit adultery; do not steal; do not lie; do not cheat; honor your father and mother.'" "Teacher," the man said, "ever since I was young I have obeyed all these commandments." With love Jesus looked straight at him and said: "You need only one thing. Go and sell all you have and give the money to the poor, and you will have riches in heaven; then come and follow me." When the man heard this, gloom spread over his face and he went away sad, because he was very rich.
>
> Jesus looked around at his disciples and said to them, "How hard it will be for rich people to enter the Kingdom of God!" The disciples were shocked at these words, but Jesus went on to say: "My children, how hard it is to enter the Kingdom of God! It is much harder for a rich man to enter the Kingdom of God than for a camel to go through the eye of a needle." At this the disciples were completely amazed, and asked one another, "Who, then, can be saved?" Jesus looked straight at them and answered: "This is impossible for men, but not for God; everything is possible for God."[6]

The young man was offered the same possibility offered to the disciples at Pentecost and to those who heard Peter and the other apostles on that occasion: the genuine possibility of repentance, of breaking with past responses to life and embracing a radical new acceptance of the unknown. The possibility, in other words, of valuing his life as good. But the young man did not do so, for "he was very rich."

Abstractly speaking, the amount of money a man has is not important. But Jesus was aware that what money represents in temporal security exercises tremendous power, a fact Janice and Henry also knew well. He knew that one does not easily give up what has been certain in the past. And the disciples knew it, too. They knew themselves to be "rich," as did the Simons. "Who, then, can be saved?" the disciples asked. The answer is another puzzle. "This is impossible for men, but not for God; everything is possible for God," i.e., for the Holy Spirit.

Both the disciples and the rich young man were presented with the Christ possibility. They accepted it; he did not. Logically, it would seem that the young man had just as much opportunity to follow Christ as anyone else. But he didn't do it. The Christ possibility didn't twist his arm, it didn't force him in any way. He made a free decision. Likewise, there was no absolutely compelling force to make the disciples, gathered after Jesus' death, receive the possibility present in him as their own. (The "fiery tongues" is a symbolic way of speaking that Luke employs after the fact.) But they did, as did the three thousand (among a presumably larger crowd) who responded to Peter's sermon. What sets the disciples and the rich young man apart are their respective decisions relative to Christ. Each of them could have decided differently. The difference between them was the Holy Spirit.

The possibility offered in Jesus Christ may not be incorporated into an already existing life pattern. By its very nature, it calls for a radical change in direction, a right-about-face in relating to life. The rich young man knew this and so did the disciples. If adopted, it means a drastic shift in the context in which all other decisions are made. It requires, in other words, death: the rejection of allegiance to the past. For the man faced with decision demanded by Christ, the death is nothing short of final; he must give up everything that has given life meaning. None of us do this lightly. Acceptance of the Christ possibility is not a casual affair.

It should not be surprising, therefore, that Christians through the centuries have longed for what Bonhoeffer called "cheap grace," decision for the Christ possibility without death. They have longed for human existence without the necessity of receiving the full complement of life. They have longed for the gift of life apart from the giver of life—the absolute limits and impossible demands. They have, in other words, longed for Christ without the Holy Spirit, the hard decision to receive the Christ possibility in its entirety. But real life just isn't that way. The Grand Inquisitor offered demonic salvation to his people, and so have his descendants ever since.

As a man contemplates the decision to follow Christ, he weighs the consequences, as he does with every major decision. Does what he stands to gain weigh heavier than what he stands to lose? As he contemplates his own life he cannot condemn the rich young man, who stood to lose a great deal that was certain, only to gain a future composed of uncertain perils—the very perils from which his wealth protected him.

When the Pentecost story is placed beside the one about the rich young man, a frightening element of human existence cannot fail to come home. A human being is free. That is, he is under no compulsion to choose either this or that when it comes to deciding who is to be his Lord, what is to be the operating mode of his life. And moreover, there is no authority to which he can apply for certainty that the decision will be right. A man's longing for certainty of the rightness of his decision, and the consequent refusal to decide when that certainty fails to appear, is what Janice Simon meant when she identified her life prior to the decision to move as hell. Many a man has viewed the Christ offering of total freedom as hell. Bonhoeffer pointed to this absolute freedom when he noted that "the responsible man acts in the freedom of his own self, without the *support* of men, circumstances or principles, but with a due consideration for the given human and general conditions and for the relevant questions of principle."[7] When the chips are down, a man knows he—and he alone—must make the decision relative to the Christ possibility, the existential possibility of being free as he stands before the absolute limits and impossible demands that comprise his human existence.

When faced with Christ, no man can fail to make a decision. Either he decides for life (as he knows and wishes it) or he decides for death (as he knows and fears it). The necessity of decision, so the testimony of those who have gone before declares, is genuine freedom. But, it must be reiterated, genuine freedom, when seen in the offing, looks like the end of everything, as anything but desirable. The only evidence to the contrary is the testimony of those who have gone that path. Nothing in one's past history would suggest such—life under the sign of Christ is a radically new and different world of relationships with oneself, other people and things, and with God. The symbol of that life is a cross.

The Christ possibility may be a possibility, then, but it is an absurd one. A man would be a fool to make it his own. But the Christ possibility doesn't ask about foolishness or wisdom. It boldly asks for a decision—choose death and hell or choose life and heaven. No other options are present and no support is available for the lonely individual as he faces the necessity of decision. But built into the possibility of life is the command that it be chosen as one's own. "The commandment of God is the permission to live as man before God. . . . It differs from all human laws in that it commands freedom."[8]

A man is not compelled to obey the command of God, but when he decides to do so, there is the Holy Spirit, the symbol of life everlasting. "You must realize," Paul wrote to the Corinthians, "that no one who is led by God's Spirit can say, 'A curse on Jesus!', and no one can confess 'Jesus is Lord,' unless he is guided by the Holy Spirit."[9]

The Accountable Life

The tradition in Christian history that has insisted "once saved always saved" has failed to take seriously the fact that once a man has elected Christ as his Lord, as the operating mode of his life, the necessity of constant life decisions has but begun. Far from putting an end to excruciating decisions, acceptance of the Christ possibility lays upon a man the terrible demand to remake the decision for genuine life at every turn.

An ancient story has Joshua speaking to the Assembly of Israel at Shechem.[10] "Choose this day," he tells the gathered People, "whom you will serve. Either you will serve the Gods your fathers worshiped beyond the river or the gods in whose land you dwell. But as for me and my house, we will serve Yahweh." The People responded, in what was obviously a traditional response, "We will serve Yahweh." When Joshua declared the decision to be no simple one, that Yahweh was a jealous God, they yet insisted they would serve Yahweh. Joshua then put it bluntly. "See that rock over there?" he said in effect. "It has heard every word you have said, that you would serve Yahweh. It will stand in judgment upon you that you will serve Yahweh." And the People responded, "We will serve Yahweh."

I have often been impressed with this story as one of the most remarkable in the Old Testament. Joshua made the assembled People come to terms with the fact that they would be *accountable* for the decision they made. They would have to answer for their faithfulness to the decision. Joshua assumed that Yahweh would answer back (judgment) to failure to keep the promise to serve him. The People were taking a gigantic step, one that could not simply be reversed. It was a decision that could possibly be their own destruction, should they fail actually to keep allegiance to the God of Abraham, Isaac, and Jacob. The destruction, Joshua made clear, was not external to themselves. The destruction would be their own doing—as a result of refusal to keep the promise.

The promise made at Shechem by the People of Israel rested upon the historical knowledge of the promise they understood to have been given them by Yahweh: "I will be your God; you will be my people." It was, further, the promise that the people would multiply (a genuine concern of ancient tribal man) and fill the earth, and subdue it. It was the promise that, although Israel was but a speck among the peoples of the earth, it would step into history, calling all men to acknowledge and affirm the life understanding that bore the name Yahweh.

For the early church, the promise, while related to the promise to Israel, took a different form: "You will receive the gift of the Holy Spirit." The context of this promise is not the same as the Old Testament context. Instead of being issued to a people, the promise of the Holy Spirit is given to every man who repents and is baptized in the name of Jesus the Messiah. The promise, therefore, is for whoever, be he "Jew" or "Greek," will decide to choose Christ as the operating mode of his life.

We should be clear at this point that the Holy Spirit is not a prize held out to those who repent. When Peter in his sermon said, "Repent . . . and you will receive the gift of the Holy Spirit," he did not mean that the Holy Spirit would follow upon repentance.[11] He did not say, "Repent, and *then* you will receive the gift of the Holy Spirit." Instead, he pointed to the testimonial fact that a man's decision to receive the Christ possibility is the Holy Spirit, "God in him."

As is the case with all symbols, the Holy Spirit must be approached from several directions. Not only is the Holy Spirit a man's decision to obey the command of God in Christ, it also is the promise that he will always in the future make the same decision. As the ancient Hebrew was called to promise that he would serve Yahweh, who promised to him the filling of the earth, the man confronted with the Christ possibility is called to respond to the promise that life will always be good. The fitting or corresponding promise on his part is that he will always receive all that is, all that comes to him as his life, as a gift, as good. The decision to receive the Christ possibility is simultaneously the decision to be accountable for remaking the decision at every turn of daily existence.

Joshua's admonition to Israel is still an admonition to men today: You cannot decide to let Christ be the operating mode of your life—it's too hard and involves consequences you may very well not want to receive. But the People's answer is also demanded of men today: We will choose life—our life—as good, now and always. And, just as Joshua did not pressure the People to serve Yahweh, Christ does not pressure modern man to receive him. The decision to promise is a totally free decision, and in so being is the gift of the Holy Spirit, the decision of God. "The free deed," Bonhoeffer wrote, "knows itself in the end as the deed of God; the decision knows itself as guidance; the free venture knows itself as divine necessity."[12] Looking into the future, the man called to repentance, called on to make promises, called on to decide the direction his life will take, finds no absolute assurance, nothing that will take the decision from him or soften the impact of its consequences. But looking backward after the decision, he is given to know that his decision was correlated to the demand to make the decision in the first place.

The accountable man, then, is completely willing to bear the consequences of whatever life brings. He trusts that what the future holds is good—even though there may be reason to suspect it will be unpleasant or even terrifying. He acts without certain knowledge of consequences, though possible consequences are taken into consideration. Bonhoeffer noted that the proof of what he called the responsible man's freedom "is the fact that nothing can answer for him, nothing can exonerate him, except his own deed and his own self."[13] Accountability includes the refusal to lay blame or credit on anyone or anything—including, especially, God—for one's own beliefs, ideas, actions; in a word, for one's own life.

To assume such radical accountability is to recognize the social character of the individual man. Men today commonly recognize that they are what they do, where they exist, and with whom they associate. A man becomes who he is by recognizing himself as the point at which a whole host of relationships intersect, yet identifiably separate from the subjects of any relationship.

In assuming accountability for his own life, a man simultaneously assumes accountability for the lives of all with whom he lives related, and increasingly it is becoming apparent that no spot exists where a man may escape relationship with every other man. The radical accountability that bears the symbolic name Holy Spirit, then, entails suffering—the taking into one's own conscious being the beings of other men and things. And that means nothing short of assuming the consequences of other men's actions. In so doing, "Man is summoned to share in God's sufferings at the hands of a godless world."[14]

"God's sufferings" are all but incomprehensible to modern man. Let us play a game. The world population is now in excess of three billion people. And God is supposed to have the hairs of the heads of each one numbered. Even our computerized technology is confounded at the concept. Add all the animals and birds and rocks and trees, and the mind of God becomes a vast repository of irrelevant data. When we stop playing games, however, the symbol of God's numbering of hairs alters in character. The myth allows us to grasp the reality that nothing is unimportant, that though we must for pragmatic reasons eliminate from our conscious consideration most elements of our existence, they are not thereby insignificant.

When we speak of the sufferings of God in this context, therefore, we point to the absolute goodness of each minute speck of creation. And, further, we point to the possibility of human openness to the most unimportant event that transpires. For the man who so participates in the suffering of God, everything that happens

79532

happens to him, and everything that will happen will happen to him. Nothing is excluded. And that, by anyone's definition, is suffering. But accountability is much more than an abstract openness to all events in human history. Accountability is the assumption of the consequences of those events, including all those over which a man has no direct control.

If the gift of the Holy Spirit is the gift of suffering and accountability present in a man's decision to receive the possibility of life's goodness, it is also the gift of real joy in accountability and suffering. Joy is a central theme in the Christian faith. It points to the jubilation, the passion, present in the reception of the Christ possibility. The Christian is a peculiar bird. He joys in the midst of war and trouble. He sings in the midst of anxiety. He acts in contradistinction to those "realists" who "face boldly" the evil in the world. In the face of evil, he laughs. In so doing, he not only shows up as a fool, but declares the realists to be foolish, for the realist takes evil to be the reality of the world, whereas the gift of the Holy Spirit is the gift of constantly deciding to receive life and the world as unalterably good, and evil either a misreading of life or a perversion of it. The gift of the Holy Spirit lies in saying yes to all of life—and doing so through definite action. The Holy Spirit, therefore, finally is man's reduplication in historical action of his decision for the Christ possibility.

Reduplicating the Decision

A curious story appears in the Gospel according to Matthew of Jesus' demand that his disciples walk on water. They were out in a boat fishing, and here came Jesus walking toward them as though on dry land. Rather preposterous in itself—and so the disciples thought. It must be a disembodied spirit, it certainly couldn't be a man. Then Jesus identified himself—and they knew *him* to be a human being. Suddenly he invited them to be human beings, too. He invited them to meet him out on the water. Peter got out of the boat, took a few steps, and sank. Many contemporary men could tell the same story. They have decided for the Christ possibility and then have chickened out. They begin to wonder if it

LINCOLN CHRISTIAN COLLEGE AND SEMINARY

might not have been better to stay with what was certain. After all, the unknown future is mighty frightening.

The story of the solid water suggests another pointer toward the Holy Spirit: action that brings the decision for Christ into history. An old revival hymn speaks of the "power in the blood of the Lamb." We have been led to believe this power is efficacious for saving men from the vicissitudes of life. But, no, it is power of an entirely different order. It is a man's decisive action in walking on the water. It is the action of stepping out into life unprotected by any self-defense.

Water has long symbolized the unknown. Ancient man looked out to sea and saw a vast expanse where he could not go and from which came terrible monsters to devastate him and his creations. From the Gilgamesh Epic to Homer to Beowulf to modern tales of unknown monsters in the ocean depths, the myth has grown apace.

A look at two Old Testament stories will reveal the opportunity for decisive action that water has been understood to occasion. In the Noah story it is God—not fate or evil force—that raises the waters over the earth. The devastating force is God himself. But—note carefully—it is also God who conquers the waters, who instructs Noah to build the ark. The story has Noah fully aware that his contemporaries would consider him a fool to construct his large boat. Yet, despite the threat of ostracism (always a primal threat for ancient man; witness, e.g., *Oedipus Rex*), he proceeded with his building. He obeyed the command of God. What we have in the Noah story is dramatization of the God activity that is met both in the unknown and in the action that challenges the unknown. That challenging action is the Holy Spirit.

The second biblical story tells of the Hebrew exodus from Egypt. Water forms the absolute limit to the Hebrew People's flight from Pharaoh. At the Red Sea[15] the People of Israel met God himself. The water cut them off from their hope of freedom. Again, God calls on the People to challenge the absolute limit to life. Moses walked to the brink—and the waters parted, letting the People pass. Such charging the barrier in trust of the barrier is the Holy Spirit.

The Gospel writers were quite familiar with Noah and Exodus.

Who has control over the "wind and the waves"?[16] God does. Who demands that man walk on the waters, venture into the unknown, risk life and limb in the impossible? God does. From the point beyond which man cannot go comes the demand that man proceed into the impossible.

The human being approaching the disciples' boat gave no assurances that, should they elect to join him in the unknown, he would hold them up. He simply called them to come out. In other words, Jesus offered no guarantee of success. He demanded, on the other hand, absolute trust, responsible decision—and promised that with the decision came the possibility of its reduplication in action. Jesus' own presence on the water was testimony to the possibility of doing what the disciples were called on to decide to do.

These stories from ancient lore are really not ancient at all. They are as contemporary as this month's Book of the Month selection. They speak of action, action relative to the wild forces that box man in, that present him with terrifying and insurmountable obstacles. These stories talk—can it be?—of God handing to man the power exercised by God himself. They speak of the Holy Spirit.

The Holy Spirit is a man's historical action corresponding to his decision to receive the Christ possibility. It is his embodiment of the decision to say yes to the possibility offered in Christ. It is walking into the unknown unafraid. It is a man's active assumption that he is lord of the forces of insecurity, past actions, and external circumstances. It is trust translated into deeds, trust that receives the present and future as good, in the secure knowledge that the past is the great, good gift of God—no matter what it might have been. The Holy Spirit is action that demonstrates affirmation of life without qualification. The Holy Spirit is the deed of a man who responds through Christ to God, who presents men with their own existence and demands that they be accountable for it. God calls a man to live on his own. Christ offers the possibility of living free. The Holy Spirit is a man's free decisive action. The Holy Spirit is a man walking on the water, a man reduplicating the Christ possibility.

The problem for men is, and always has been, to reduplicate their decision to receive the Christ possibility. Deciding to be free is relatively easy, but acting on the decision is another matter, as Peter demonstrated when he got out of the boat. It is difficult because the Holy Spirit action requires a trust men find infinitely threatening. Human beings are presented with the demand to master the wind and the seas, the storms of cybernation, racial strife, and international war. They are called to master emotional conflict, family tension, personal insecurity. Men are not asked to eliminate war and insecurity; only to master them. They, the "powers," are to be men's servants, not men theirs. War, insecurity, automation are to work for men. Men are not to work for them. But men do not always wage war to secure peace, automation is used to make automatons of persons, and insecurity is harnessed to make men slaves. Men have taken the great, good gifts of God and submitted themselves in servitude to them. As Peter, they have stepped out into the unknown and, becoming afraid, have sunk. Having chosen to receive all of life as good, they have refused to reduplicate the decision in action. They have refused the awful responsibility of receiving the gift of life to be used by them. Embodiment of the Holy Spirit, reduplication of the decision for Christ, requires courage: the courage to rush the absolute barriers of life, the courage to challenge God himself. In the Holy Spirit, men assume the responsibility of God in the world.

Fully aware that he cannot secure his own significance, much less his existence, a man acting out the Christ possibility drives directly into what comes as limit to his life, setting aside anxiety or fear (although taking them fully into account). He does so fully expecting the barriers to fall before him, as the sea opened for the Hebrews and the ark floated for Noah and the water supported Peter. His charge is the Holy Spirit.

But charging the barriers is a dangerous business. Challenging God can come perilously close to rebellion against God—sin. But there exists, in Kierkegaard's term, an "infinite qualitative difference" between them. And that difference lies in the challenging man's trust in what he challenges, as contrasted with the rebellious man's rejection of that against which he rebels. In charging the barriers, a man knows full well that the barriers may not fall—and joyfully takes the hard lump when they do not, only to get up and discern the new and different barriers now before him for challenging. The Holy Spirit life is faithful, hopeful, and open.

A SUMMARY NOTE

The Trinity may now be seen as a unified symbol of life as it actually is, instead of ancient magic or double (triple) talk. For contemporary men the three persons of the Trinity are symbolic ways of apprehending the reality of their relationships with the world around them—and at the same time affirming a particular character for that relationship.

It is impossible to exhaust the scope of the Trinitarian symbol. "God," "Christ," and "Holy Spirit" cannot be replaced by synonyms. But I have suggested that at least they point toward the following:

God—the absolute limits and impossible demands that appear in a man's consciousness as his definition.

Christ—the possibility of receiving the absolute limits and impossible demands as good and for my good. In Christ, a man has no particular knowledge of the intrinsic character of the persons and events around him. He has only the possibility of receiving them *as* good. Christ is a response to life, and, as such, speaks of the character of a man's relationship to men and things, not necessarily of the nature of men and things.

Holy Spirit—the decision to receive the Christ possibility as the operating mode (Lord) of one's life; the promise always to so receive life as good; and the active reduplication of the decision and promise in historical existence.

The three symbols are inseparable. A man cannot say "God," except through the possibility that bears the name "Christ," which name is only a pious or magical cant without the decisive and promissorial action that is the Holy Spirit. The three are tied together also in a more formal way: the demand of God is close to the life possibility offered in Christ; the possibility in Christ is close to the decision of the Holy Spirit; and the action of the Holy Spirit is with reference to the limit of God. The Trinity is one. The Trinity is life as it actually is.

Despite those who, by reason of failure to comprehend the contemporary significance of the Trinity, would replace or discard the Apostles' Creed, the Creed remains the basic historical affirmation of life under the Trinitarian symbol. Like the biblical witness, the Apostles' Creed must constantly be reunderstood. The creed that follows is therefore not submitted as a substitute for the historic Creed, but as a way of reunderstanding it.

A CREED FOR THE SECULAR SAINT

I trust myself to the absolute limits and impossible demands that define my life and call me to live its full definition; and commit myself to the reception and declaration of the possibility of life's goodness and death's goodness that is presented for my choosing from outside my consciousness and remains external in my history as a constant possibility;

And I gratefully embody my decision for self affirmation, number myself among those who live the free life; know I am significant; and hope ever to be momentarily renewed in this trust, in the sure awareness that my self is important throughout time.

III

The Action

5

The Secular Saint

WE ARE TRANSMITTERS

As we live, we are transmitters of life.
And when we fail to transmit life, life fails to flow through us.

That is part of the mystery of sex, it is a flow onwards.
Sexless people transmit nothing.

And if, as we work, we can transmit life into our work,
life, still more life, rushes into us to compensate, to be ready,
and we ripple with life through the days.

Even if it is a woman making an apple dumpling, or a man a stool,
if life goes into the pudding, good is the pudding,
good is the stool,
content is the woman, with fresh life rippling into her,
content is the man.

Give, and it shall be given unto you
is still the truth about life.
But giving life is not so easy.
It doesn't mean handing it out to some mean fool, or letting the living
     dead eat you up.
It means kindling the life-quality where it was not,
even if it's only in the whiteness of a washed pocket-handkerchief.

                                        D. H. LAWRENCE

ONCE A MAN has elected the Christ response to the God activity in decisive action of the Holy Spirit, what then? What specific activity is in keeping with the Christ decision? Jesus' answer to the young man who asked "What must I do . . . ?" is instructive. He asked after the context in which his interrogator raised the question. Do you know the rules? Yes, he was told, I know and have obeyed them since I was a little tyke. Only then did Jesus answer the original question directly. You must, he said in effect, decide to be free of the bondage in which you live. You must decide to stop hiding from life. But the words came out in terms of the specifics of the young man's existence—Jesus cut to the heart of his bondage. It was an answer tailored for the situation, which is the only relevant answer possible. Since general answers cannot be provided for the highly individual question "What must I do?", what follows suggests a minimal action context for Secular Saints. It is certainly not exhaustive and is not intended to be prescriptive. Secular Saints are free from allegiance to any particulars, including those outlined below; nevertheless, a reasoned discussion of how a Secular Saint looks is urgently needed. What might such a man do and be?

The Self: A Relationship Matrix

A Secular Saint is a self. In recent years a great deal of discussion has centered about the "concept of the self." And what it comes to is an attempt to understand the Secular Saint in the aspect of his personal life-style, of the way he relates himself to the persons and things around him. There is no question of *whether* he relates himself to the surrounding human and material environment. No one can avoid that, even if he wishes to do so. The question is *how?* and the how depends largely upon what he considers the world around to be.

I have been in countless group sessions that began with "Let's all go around and introduce ourselves." Deadly as this ritual usually is, the form of the self-introduction is instructive for understanding the self. Each one introduces himself—reveals his self—by placing his life in relation to other people and things. He tells of his family, immediate and/or parental; where he lives, and where he used to live; where he works and at what; what he enjoys when he is not working; where he went to school; what clubs he belongs to; etc. He is, so he says, the complex of relationships he outlines, and he is able to assume that the outline will be meaningful to his hearers because it is similar, at least in form, to their own, and because it may (and certainly would if the list were sufficiently extended) overlap their own complex of relationships. In other words, it is possible to present oneself to others because it is possible to enter their relationship matrix or self. Perhaps one of the reasons the little green men from Mars hold such fascination for earthlings is that they are entirely outside of any known relationship matrix, which also explains the fear of an invasion from outer space.

No one introduces himself in terms of his chemical and biological constituency, and should he do so he would be considered by himself and others to be a jokester. For by so doing, he would not be presenting him*self*, he would be describing an object. A self, as opposed to a thing, *is* his relationship with the world around him. But things, too, are defined by their relationship with the surrounding world. The desk upon which I write is what it is by virtue of its relationship with me, just as I am defined by my relation with it. Its relationship matrix is equally as extensive and complex as my own. Its history is equally unique.

But the desk is not a self and does not have the potential of becoming a self—because the desk cannot choose the character of a single one of its relationships. The desk is constituted by actions totally external to it. The self, on the other hand, chooses the character of all his relationships, including the most distant and unknown. Note: the self does not choose the subjects of every relationship; he chooses the character of them all. He decides, in other words, how he will relate to his world. As we have seen, there are two fundamental ways of relating to life: sin and Christ; as bad and as good, as against me and for me. These are alternative choices for the character of the relationship matrix that comprises the self.

But the self is not really a self in the sin response to life, for sin is a refusal to engage in relations with those parts of the relationship matrix that do not match a prescribed image. This decision is impossible to implement, however, because the world around does not go away. Whether a man wishes it or not, he is of necessity related to everyone and everything. Denying that fact makes the fact no less real. Sin could be called a possible impossibility. It is obviously possible because men consistently elect it; it is impossible because it cannot be accomplished. The church has given sin its proper name: death—not living as a self, but living in the effort to be a thing, which is not a genuine option for human beings.

The Christ decision about relating to the world around, on the other hand, chooses every relationship to be good and for me. It makes a value judgment on the subjects of these relationships, a judgment that allows them, indeed, wills them to be part of the self. And, simultaneously, the Christ decision wills that the self enter the relationship matrix of the subjects of his own relationships, which he knows to be everyone and everything in the created universe, including little green men. By opting for the Christ response to life, the self becomes the self and thereby chooses to tie in with the world as it actually is. Therein lies a clue to the context in which "What must I do?" may be existentially answered.

Saint Paul wrote to the Corinthians, when he learned they were perverting the word of freedom, that, indeed, "all things are lawful for me, but not all things are helpful."[1] Without attempting to exegete Paul's meaning, I wish to take his formula and alter a few words in an effort to suggest a beginning point for the life of the twentieth-century Christ-man—the Secular Saint.

"Everything is permitted; but not everything is necessary." Everything is permitted—we are free from the law, absolutely free. Nothing is required, nothing is demanded. And therein lies the terror of the Christian faith, for when everything is permitted, a man is left only with his own free decision about what he will do (which is the same as who he will be). He is free to do whatever he wills to do.

The fear of those who live before a God who permits some things and denies others is that the radically liberating word will lead to uncontrolled license, by which they mean repeated violation of the taboos established by their own system. When such violation occurs, they know themselves to be vitally endangered, although often they are unaware of the point of real danger.

Seldom does the man of fear properly identify license as participation in unnecessary activity. In order to do so he would have to recognize the ways in which the necessary is made known. And that is possible only when everything is permitted. The necessary appears only when a man permits an other to enter his own life. No necessity rears its head so long as a man insists on living within his own self, for the self can create its own self only through the exclusion of the necessary. The necessary is, by definition, exterior to the self. It is that over which the self has no control.

License is the dedication of the self to activity that is outside the necessary, indeed to activity that rejects the necessary. It is activity, in other words, that denies the validity of the necessary's claim upon him. License, far from permitting everything, permits only the activity that keeps the necessary at arm's length.

What does the licentious man prohibit his self? He prohibits the claim of the other to reach him, as is clearly evident in the playboy who operates on the assumption that women are playmates to be utilized at his whim, just as his sports car. Not only does he deny women the right to their own selfhood—which he cannot do, of course, unless they allow him—but he denies himself the freedom of being his own self by refusing to allow the selfhood of the other (in this case the women he selects) to condition his own existence.

The antithesis of the licentious man is the Secular Saint, who is able to respond to whatever presents itself, able to receive into his self everything that comes from the other. Everything includes both pleasure and pain, both birth and death, each little bit of which the Secular Saint receives as the goodness of his life. His life comes from the other, which forms the definition of his life.

A few months before his death in the crash of a Boeing 727 jetliner, Carl Michalson of Drew University addressed a gathering sponsored by the Faith and Culture Institute in Washington, D.C. Outlining the way the faithful man relates to the specifics of his existence, he cited a passenger in an airplane that suddenly developed engine trouble and began rapidly to lose altitude. At times such as this, so goes the myth, men see their lives pass before their eyes and promptly repent of their evil and thoughtless deeds. But the man of faith, Michalson said, finds himself with a far different problem. His question, as the plane nears the ground, is: "Have I paid the premium on my life-insurance policy?" By so doing, he not only affirms the goodness of his impending death, but also affirms himself as the socially responsible self he is.

The Secular Saint receives his death as good just as he receives his birth as good. After all, he has no more experience of life before he was born than he does of life following his death. Birth and death are the absolute limits to his existence and, as such, are equally received as good gifts. Only in sin, the faithless act of thinking life can be lived only on his own terms, does a man reject his death as bad. The Secular Saint does not, of course, court death; after all, he does not set his own limits and their times. But when they come he takes them with open arms—even his *own* death. I once heard a clergyman declare sermonically that he hoped never to be duped by a doctor who wanted to hide from him his impending death, because he did not want to be cheated out of this final consciousness. This was the statement of a Secular Saint who was choosing to allow every part of his self to be conscious to him.

The question about insurance premiums reveals another element in the response of the Secular Saint to the absolute limit of his impending death. When he dies, the Secular Saint causes alterations in the selves of many other people.

The insurance premium question is an acknowledgment of that fact, nothing more nor less; obviously, he cannot then and there write out and mail a neglected payment. But the awareness that he is the responsible subject of relationships that comprise the selves of others is a major part of his own selfhood; when he dies, others are changed, a fact that is most obvious when his wife, children, friends, and co-workers are recognized as part of his self's definition. In receiving his own death as good, therefore, the Secular Saint also receives drastic change in the lives of others as good— and trusts their new selves without him to be brand new gifts to them, that will include, he hopes, his life-insurance benefits.

The licentious man or the man of sin cannot allow the other

selves that limit and place demands upon him to intrude upon his self definition as death approaches. He cannot receive the complexity of his selfhood when his consciousness itself is ultimately threatened. He is not, therefore, genuinely free, for he rejects the necessary—which always confronts him in highly concrete forms, such as a failing airplane engine.

But surely no one can fail to face the necessary when it appears as the ground coming up toward him. Ah, but he can. He can fail to respond to the necessary in the demand to be accountable for his family, his colleagues, his friends. Only the Secular Saint can live with the guilt of being licentious (as he knows he is, despite his decision to the contrary). And in so doing he can live free before the necessary as it rushes toward him while he sits strapped in an airplane seat. He can trust the immediate, unexpected necessary as the goodness of his life, permitting the selfhood of other selves to condition his response to his own death.

The decision to live before the word, "everything is permitted," is the decision to allow, indeed insist, that the selfhood of the other determine the content of what is permitted, the content of freedom itself. The desires of the other self are not the content of necessity, but his self, his humanness, is, and the necessity present in the other is the other's need to reject license and embrace free accountability. The man of permission and necessity—the Secular Saint— is the man for others, with others, and in others.

From the perspective of total permission and absolute necessity, it is possible to understand precisely those who are most "moral" to be licentious—for they engage in unnecessary activity, activity that is designed to limit the impact of other selves upon their own. The moralist, for example, who refuses to enter establishments that feature blue entertainment—and if he does, refuses to enjoy himself—is attempting to block part of his self out of his self, which is the meaning of licentiousness. He declines to admit the immoral into his life, and to that extent is no longer free. By labeling an other immoral, the moralist indicates his refusal to allow that other to be part of his own self—and at the same time indicates his desire not to be part of the self of that other. The necessary, however, lies precisely in the opposite direction, for—whether the moralist wishes it or not—the other is part of his self definition. The Secular Saint, who chooses to be his necessary self, knows that his self is defined by the selves of others; what happens to those selves and the degree to which they are characterized by permission or freedom is thus vitally important to him: their selves are his self.

No less than the keeper of the moral law, the violator of the law may be engaged in unnecessary deeds. Since the necessary lies in the claim of the other's selfhood, the violator of the law runs the grave risk of avoiding the value the law is intended to maintain. Much has been made in recent years of civil disobedience on the part of civil-rights and peace advocates. Blanket condemnations have been issued by proponents of law and order and cautious seals of approval have been tendered by church and civil libertarian groups. Usually those involved in the disobedience have been clear about the fact they were violating not only the law of the land but also the moral code of the community. Blocking traffic on major roadways and sitting on airport runways has been justified by appeal to a higher law than those violated.

There is no assurance that these acts are not licentious, just as there is no assurance they are. The real possibility cannot be ruled out, however, that these acts fail to affirm the selfhood of those inconvenienced in the process. They are ostensively designed to enhance the selfhood of culturally deprived persons, but the universality of the self may well be denied in so doing: the possibility of free response to their lives is not necessarily offered to stalled motorists and airline passengers, and may not be offered to the impoverished the acts are intended to benefit. Once more, these acts may be efforts to limit the involvement of the protesters in the lives of those they are affecting. The Secular Saint takes the selfhood of every known person into serious consideration when he acts, and takes upon himself the guilt of cutting out some while affirming others. He does not act in anger—though anger may be present—but acts always in the sorrowful awareness that he and his fellows constantly deny their own selfhood in their violation of the law. In sum, the Secular Saint takes upon himself the responsibility for his lawless activity, being always eager to bear the consequences of what he does. The necessary is still the selfhood of the other—each other—his actions affect, and violation of law is no more assurance of adherence to the necessary than is adherence to the law.

The real question before those who would be disobedient to the law is: Are my actions offering the possibility of free selfhood to as many components of my own self as possible? And when this question is answered in the affirmative, he nevertheless must confess himself to be licentious. Is this particular violation in keeping with the necessary? Maybe—or maybe not. The Secular Saint is left to judge for himself.

The Secular Saint lives in the constant tension between total permission or absolute freedom and ironclad necessity or complete obligation. Such a life is far more taxing than a life lived in either permission alone (license) or necessity alone (bondage). Its difficulty lies, on the one hand, in the lack of secure guidelines that may be kept, which make it unnecessary for a man to make his own decisions (the rule decides for him). On the other hand, the lack of accepted norms for behavior is equally terrifying to the licentious man, who is thus presented with the impossibility of having no rule to violate.

As we have seen, the licentious man chooses to limit the definition of his self to the relationships he deems pleasurable, without regard for the self of the other. He lives, nevertheless, within society, which has developed social norms designed to govern intraself relationships. That these norms often become barriers to selfhood in no way alleviates the validity of such norm systems. The Secular Saint is aware of the social norms but chooses to live free of them—which does not mean he ignores them or refuses to abide by them. They are simply subject to his choosing, as is every other aspect of his life.

But the licentious man is unable to sit loose to social norm systems. They come to him as binding principles, just as they do to the moralist. As the necessary, they must be rejected *because* they demand considerate relationships with the other, *because* they demand that the other be the definition of his own self. But what if there were no law to violate? The licentious man would find himself in the situation that is freely chosen by the Secular Saint: he would have to choose his own relationship characteristics. In a society that insists upon formal monogamous sexual relationships, for example, the licentious man can reject this norm with certainty; he can know the rules he violates—and can derive some degree of pleasure in violating them, justifying himself by thinking the law is all he violates.

Long ago, Paul put his finger on the licentious man when he charged that some of his followers, thinking the law was null and void, could disregard their fellows by their own gluttony while others starved. Freedom from the law pure and simple is license, unconcern for the other, but Paul was very clear that "the law is holy, and right, and good."[2] Paul knew that the law was what made his knowledge of sin possible. Likewise, the licentious man in the twentieth century needs the law in order to be a licentious man. Without it, he is left to his own devices, his own judgment. With no law to violate, he runs the severe risk of being forced to make his own decisions, the consequences of which he would have to bear himself. The licentious man is thus tied to the moral law in order to violate it, as the moralist needs the law in order to keep it.

Only the Secular Saint is able to exist, joying in the free responsibility to make and keep (or break) his own promises. Looking eagerly into the future, he knows fully the terror of the unknown that waits there. Yet he awaits it in the secure knowledge that, whatever else it might be, the unknown is good. The mood of the Secular Saint before the future is excitement. He is ever aware that his present decisions condition the character of the future, but he knows full well that his decisions in no way determine the future. Nevertheless, he is bold to make decisions in the present as though their consequences would follow his dictates. His life is exciting in the midst of terror and anxiety, joy and hope.

Emotional Freedom

The Secular Saint not only acknowledges his emotions but enjoys them. Far from keeping them boxed in from the view of others and himself, he lets them loose, thereby participating fully in all that life brings. His model could well be Kazantzakis' Zorba, who dances at joy and dances at grief, who refuses to hesitate when life presents unwanted responsibilities and moves into them with vigor, who exults openly at pleasure. The Secular Saint receives his emotions as genuinely good.

In some strands of its tradition, the Christian church has ignored the goodness of emotion. When it has done so, it has failed to understand the exhilarating fullness of human existence, finding "pleasure" to be contrary to the gospel. Such life denial has resulted in such strange activity as suppression of the theater, dancing, card-playing, and alcohol, not to mention the pretense that sexual desire does not exist, much less is good.

Saint Paul has been cited repeatedly[3] to substantiate the church's refusal to recognize emotions. Paul spoke often of the necessity to discipline the body in order that the work of God may be done. But Paul would be a poor example of a genuinely nonemotional existence. His outbursts against the perversions of the church at Corinth, for example, illustrate his propensity for wrath, and his tenderness toward Onesimus reveals a capacity for friendship and compassion.

But what of his stern injunctions to the Corinthians about drunkenness and gluttony? These must be seen in context. Paul actually said little about what later Christians came to call vices and sins. Instead, he was concerned that his churches and their members be accountable, that they act in accordance with the reception of Christ they professed. He wanted them to assume fully the consequences of their decisions and (a matter that will be discussed in more detail later) to perform adequately the mission of proclaiming Christ in the world.

Paul was not in the least denying the goodness of emotion. He was rather calling for the mastery of emotion for the sake of the Word of Jesus Christ in the world. For Paul there was nothing to be censored in "whooping it up," but he was firm that celebration should not be at the expense of the Word—the possibility of free, accountable life.

Paul, therefore, gives twentieth-century Secular Saints a clue. The church has been right in its caution about emotions. Emotions are dangerous. They have the power to control a man to the point of relieving him of his selfhood. But the Secular Saint, by definition a self, constantly stands outside his emotions, forcing them to serve him and his mission in life. As such, the Secular Saint is heartily in favor of "fun." He finds it difficult to comprehend a Christian who is against not only sin but fun as well.

The Secular Saint is not naïve. He knows as well as any man the dangers of pleasure. He knows he is liable to the temptation to escape from life in involvement with "life." It could be, for example, that only the Christian can drink, for only the Secular Saint can allow himself the freedom to enjoy alcohol freely, yet remain master of his self. Alcohol-use is a good illustration of the place of emotion in the life of the Secular Saint, for alcohol has been named among the cardinal demons by some religious groups in recent history.

One of the objections some religious people and groups have held to the social use of alcohol is its faculty for releasing inhibitions. Under the "influence," a man may say and do things that he would normally never do. He may let down the barriers. And that is not good. A man, so say the religious objectors to alcohol, can have just as good a time with Cokes.

The Secular Saint already knows he can have a good time without alcohol. But he knows equally well he can have a good time with it. He knows there is a time to drink and a time not to drink. And he allows neither the legalism of the doctrinaire drinker nor the legalism of the dogmatic religious objector to master him. Alcohol is his servant, not he the servant of alcohol (or of any position relative to it).

But alcohol is dangerous. "No one ever starts out to be an alcoholic. He always thinks he can handle it." Of course. But the Secular Saint never depends on handling it; he knows his mastery of the demons is his own mastery through the Holy Spirit. The difference is immeasurable. There is little in life that is not dangerous, at least *in potentia*. The Secular Saint knows the danger, but lives excitingly in the midst of it, standing always on the brink of disaster—and joying in the stance. The center of his life is at the very edge of his life.

The Secular Saint is not convinced by the argument that release of emotion through artificial means is *per se* bad. He is aware that he, as all men, is conditioned by all sorts of environmental and historical factors that work against living open to the life that constantly presents itself to him. Therefore, he plunges freely into life, utilizing any avenue he chooses that allows him to sit loose to life. He welcomes everything that assists him in opening himself to life. Knowing that all parts of the created order are for his good, he receives even the gift of chemicals for the goodness of his life, while never allowing the chemicals to become the ruling passion of his existence. He is not, of course, under any obligation to consume chemicals such as alcohol at any given time or any time at all—were such the case he would no longer be free—but he does not categorically reject them either—for then he would likewise have relinquished his freedom. The Secular Saint "plays with fire," is always on the very edge of self-destruction yet, at the same time, infinitely distant from it—for he is the master of the fire, while knowing full well that the fire may rise up to conquer him.

The Secular Saint is an emotional man. He consciously involves himself with whatever engages him. He involves his whole being, allowing his responses—be they love, hate, fear, anxiety, hope, joy—to be conscious. At the same time, he is not blind to the fact that he can never know the full depth of his responses. Some, if not most, of them lie buried below his consciousness. But this hiddenness is also received as a gift by the Secular Saint. He is open to the unknown within the core of his self as he is to what comes from the periphery of that core.

Recent popular criticism of Christian worship has emphasized the fact that the validity of worship is not dependent upon the feeling that may or may not accompany the observance. The criticism, of course, is correct in noting that worship is not to be judged by any particular feeling, but the corollary assumption that emotion is not present—and important—in worship is avoided by the Secular Saint. Since he knows that his emotional response to his life, including worship services, is a significant part of who he is, he is not skittish about the good feelings he may experience in worship, but opens himself to them gladly. (He may find that worship makes him angry or sad—and these emotions are likewise received as good gifts.)

I once knew a college student who embodied the problem the Secular Saint rejects instead of seeking solutions for it. He had spent the majority of his years under the influence of religious parents and a minister who identified Christianity with "religious experience." After he had attended college for one semester, he came to me acutely disturbed because he could no longer find what he called the "presence of Christ" when he went to church. He thought his faith was weakening and was quite frightened at the prospect.

This young man had identified a particular kind of emotion with worship and was unprepared to receive himself as a person who experienced something else. His problem was how to recapture the religious emotion. The Secular Saint, on the other hand, does not isolate a particular emotion as religious and therefore superior to any other. Although he is unlikely to name any emotion as religious, he is not closed to the feelings others may so denominate. He does not, however, think anything has been proved when he has these feelings, and is under no compulsion to duplicate them under similar conditions. He is not afraid of his emotions but is equally not slave to them.

As the man who lets everything into his life, the Secular Saint could well be called a dilettante, "one who takes delight in a thing." The word dilettante has understandably come to suggest a person who dabbles irresponsibly with the arts and thus with life. After all, a man who merely enjoys a thing doesn't necessarily know much of anything about it. And if he doesn't know much about it, he may very well choose to enjoy or even construct things the experts reject. He also is likely to enjoy a whole host of things, from Beethoven to the latest pop song, from beer with Sunday afternoon TV baseball to a premiere showing of a Bergman film, from a serious discussion on foreign policy to chitchat over a card game. He is likely, in other words, to spread himself thin, moving quickly from one shallow involvement to another.

In a society such as ours, in which a premium is placed on expertise, the dilettante has scant chance of general cultural approval. The real reason for disapproval, though, lies in his refusal to settle down. Few people today settle down in the same sense their fathers did. They do not, that is, acquire a plot of land and a house and an occupation tied to proximity to the homestead. Instead, they settle down to a subject area in which they attempt to become expert. Involvement in the area of specialization may take them any place in the country or world—nevertheless, they have settled down. This description is true principally for the professional class in United States society, against which the good life is measured today. It is not measured against the old upper class of inherited wealth and certainly not against the impoverished. The middle class of the professional—the expert—is the standard.

But the Secular Saint does not settle down in any final sense. He may be a professional man who spends the bulk of his time in a limited area of interest, such as nineteenth-century English literature or the customs of a single primitive tribe or the radio waves from a distant star. But since he is open to all the future may bring, and since he is aware that he is defined in terms of his relationships with everyone and everything else, he takes delight in "all sorts and conditions of men," including those who are engaged in endeavors completely foreign to him and those who have no profession at all. He is, in other words, a dilettante.

"Dilettante" has not accumulated the meaning, "one who engages in sidelines from which he does not derive an income," as "amateur" has. Instead, it conjures up a picture of the wealthy playboy who works at nothing and is therefore free to indulge in diverse irrelevancies. There are historical reasons for this image, which come from the day when only the wealthy had the time to do anything but work from dawn to dark at income-producing activity. That the word is usually used in connection with the arts lies in the fact that, until recent years, the arts could be a free pursuit only of those who possessed wealth and the leisure that went with it.

While the eighteenth-century dilettante may well have been a gay young blade, it did by no means always follow that he was unknowledgeable of the things in which he delighted. Speaking of the young English noblemen who traveled through Europe as part of their education, J. H. Plumb notes that "the astonishing virtuosity of these young men can be seen from a recent exhibition held at

Norwich which displayed works collected on the Grand Tour during the eighteenth century, principally by the leading Norfolk families. This not only contained old masters, but also illustrated the patronage they brought to eighteenth-century Italian artists."[4] While usually extremely well educated, and highly versed in the fields to which he gave his attention, the dilettante was not a specialist, an authority, a fact Plumb makes clear. "Passionately preoccupied as tourists were with art," he writes, "few developed a keen critical judgment or displayed much independence of mind. They were willing to pay high prices for Veroneses and Titians, they prized Caravaggios and eagerly bought early Bolognese painters—Guido Reni, Guercino, and the Carraccis—artists who are now regarded as far, far inferior to Tintoretto or Botticelli, whom they consistently ignored."[5]

The twentieth-century dilettante, the Secular Saint, has no need to be a specialist, a professional, in every area of his life either. But, unlike many of his contemporaries, he is not hesitant to involve himself consciously with movements, causes, or subject areas in which he has no expert competence. He even is known to hold and express opinions on these things with the expectation that they will be heard. Certainly Martin Luther King, Jr. had this expectation when, in May of 1967, he strongly opposed the action of the United States government in Vietnam. But King, winner of the Nobel Peace Prize for his civil-rights activity, was severely criticized by both his Negro colleagues and his regular antagonists for stepping beyond the sphere of his competence and even for jeopardizing his influence for constructive change on the domestic scene. McGeorge Bundy, a foreign affairs advisor to President Lyndon B. Johnson who resigned to become president of the Ford Foundation, came to Dr. King's defense with words other Secular Saints can readily appreciate: "The right of dissent is fundamental. It includes the right to dissent even at the cost of misunderstanding and ill feeling. It emphatically includes the right of a man who is a leader in one field to express his views in another. Dr. King, for example, has every right to a public view on the war. . . ."[6] The Secular Saint retains the right to make his own judgments and take his own action, even in the face of contrary expert wisdom, always willing to be accountable for what he says and does. He takes delight in and is accountable for everything that comes his way.

Affirmation of the dilettante is particularly necessary in contemporary society because awe of the expert is widespread. "In the modern connotation," according to Hugh MacLennan, "a man trained in the classical tradition [as was the eighteenth-century dilettante] is obviously an amateur, and as such he is judged inadequate. He cannot fill a tooth, perform an abdominal, fire a rocket to the moon; he is relatively useless to the specific producer-consumer-repairer tasks which now have become nearly the whole content of life."[7] No man can possibly be expert in every field that has significant consequences for his social context, for the definition of his self. The temptation to give the facets of his existence over which he believes he has no control into the hands of the expert, therefore, is most attractive. Like every form of sin, however, this attempt to avoid responsibility finally is impossible, a fact that came home to United States citizens when atomic bombs were dropped on Japanese cities at the end of World War II.

The decision to use the weapons that were to make warfare obsolete was made by experts in science and government, but the responsibility fell upon the ordinary citizen. We dropped the bomb, and we could not avoid that fact by isolating blame on a few individuals. Why? Because those A-bombs were dropped within our own selves; men and things that formed our own definition were irrevocably altered. Each man is a different man after Hiroshima and Nagasaki than he was before.

The past is past and cannot be changed, but the future remains open. Nothing can bring back the lives and the whole limbs of fractured Japanese. But the future use or nonuse of nuclear weapons must not be relegated to the decision of experts in government alone. The nonexpert, the dilettante, is equally responsible. Do the experts advise ending a local war by nuclear means? The Secular Saint who is not a scientist has the obligation to declare himself without fear or anxiety. He knows his word is important because he is important.

The Secular Saint, however, does not hesitate to become an expert in a limited field merely because he is a dilettante. Whether he likes it or not, he cannot fail to notice that modern existence would be impossible apart from the cooperative effort of a large number of specialists who are able to increase to an extraordinary degree the general store of knowledge in a narrow field. If he is inclined in the direction of a certain specialty, and has the ability and occasion to pursue it, the Secular Saint may emerge as an expert— but without relinquishing his dilettantism. His mind roams at the same time it may concentrate on the matter immediately at hand.

Expertise, however, is not requisite to the life of the Secular Saint in the same way dilettantism is. Expertise moves in the direction of blocking out most of life in order to affirm a limited part. Dilettantism, on the other hand, moves toward opening life to the unexpected from any and all quarters, including the possibility of becoming expert in particular areas.

The Italian root of "dilettante" emphasizes "delight" or "joy." Looking wide-eyed at his life, the Secular Saint delights in what he sees. He does not simply accept or receive what comes into his present from the future; he delights in it, and in the Holy Spirit he anticipates delight in every present that is to come, whether it be pleasurable or painful, happy or sad.

The New Testament is full of injunctions to the faithful about joy. Joy for the Secular Saint is not merely the consequence of trust in God through Jesus Christ. It is commanded: rejoice, and again I say, rejoice. Rejoicing, joy, delight becomes like the love commandment: an order that cannot be obeyed.

Like love, joy may be enacted even when it is not felt, for joy is not a feeling but a way of relating to all of life, be it happy or sad. The Secular Saint conducts himself joyfully even in the midst of pain. Joy for him is thus obviously something other than happiness or pleasure, for he knows joy to be present in a man's decision to find everything that comes to be good. It is present in his decision to trust life, not only as it is, but as it will be. It is the emotional corollary to trust, to life in the Holy Spirit.

The Christmas hymn "Joy to the World" affirms that joy is present as a possible operating mode of existence. "Joy to the world, the Lord is come. Let earth receive her king." To receive the king, the Christ possibility, is equally to receive joy. But, again, joy is not merely present as a consequence of trust in God through Jesus Christ; joy is still a demand upon the Secular Saint. The mandatory character of joy is present in the dilettante element of Secular Sainthood. When the Secular Saint wills that pain, misfortune, castastrophe—as well as pleasurable events—be his own, he decides to delight in them at the same time. A man cannot be a contemporary dilettante unless he delights in everything.

I can hear the screams already: "This Secular Saint you talk about is nothing but a hedonist. Worse, he is a masochist." Not so; the Secular Saint knows the vital difference between joy and pleasure. Hedonism and masochism refer directly to pleasure and pain. But joy and delight point to the basic life mode of the Secular Saint. They point to his secure awareness that nothing can "separate us from the love of Christ."[8] Neither pleasure nor pain has any effect on his joy.

Unreserved Living

The Secular Saint does not live a life that is psychologically isolated from what goes on around him. Instead, he lives entirely open to what comes to him in life. He enters fully into every historical engagement. In the course of a bull session during one of the annual meetings of the Associated Church Press, the professional organization for Protestant periodical editors, someone commented that he had a difficult time making the decision to publish articles he felt should be made public but which he knew his publisher would not approve and many of his readers would decry. Should he go ahead and publish them, he ran the real risk of losing his job, but if he did not, he ran the risk of failing what he considered his responsibility to tell the truth as he saw it.

The editor was surprised at the quick diversity of response by his colleagues. Some declared that such decisions should always be made in favor of the publisher's position. After all, the magazine was his organ and the editor should respect that fact. Others were adamant that the truth should be presented and that it takes precedent over all other considerations.

As the conversation proceeded, however, each side modified its position as various editors confessed that they had, on occasion, tempered their original intentions because of pressure from the ecclesiastical authorities, and, on other occasions, had taken that pressure seriously but had gone ahead nevertheless. "But," said the man who had initially raised the issue, "how do you handle the anxiety that comes when you *know* the boom is going to be lowered after the mag's in the mail?" He did not receive a satisfactory answer, simply because there is none for the man who must have absolute assurances, who refuses to admit the anxiety as the goodness of his life. The gist of the group's response was that the anxiety had to be lived with. Period. And the censure had to be received. Period. But what if he lost his job? That, he was told, was one of those things. Would the world come to an end if he did?

This particular editor was struggling with a problem that all Secular Saints know only too well. Unless a man has built psychological walls about himself, never putting himself into ambiguous positions (they will come up anyway, but he can try), the possibility of anxiety and failure is constantly present as he opens himself to the activity of other selves. The Secular Saint ventures nothing without knowing that genuine possibility—but he ventures nevertheless. And he is always willing to receive the failure of his efforts (which he knows as God) as good—and rejoices in it. His model is Zorba, or, better still, Jesus, who said, "not my will but thine be done."

In his letter dated 21 July 1944, Bonhoeffer declared: "One must abandon every attempt to make something of oneself, whether it be a saint, a converted sinner, a churchman (a so-called priestly type!) a righteous man or an unrighteous one, a sick man or a healthy one."[9] He could have added "a Democrat or Republican, a Methodist or Episcopalian, a businessman or a bum, a pacifist or a warrior, an integrationist or a segregationist, a teetotaler or an alcoholic." The list is endless. The Secular Saint, in other words, has no image to which he tries to make his life conform, no picture of success or meaning by which he attempts to justify his existence. He lives free.

Bonhoeffer continued, "By this-worldliness I mean living unreservedly in life's duties, problems, successes and failures, experiences and perplexities." Stoicism? Hardly. This letter was written the day after the attempt to assassinate Hitler failed, the attempt to which Bonhoeffer devoted his efforts for months preceding his arrest and with which many of his closest friends and relatives were involved, an involvement he knew would probably mean their imprisonment and death. There can be little doubt that he knew full well, also, the grave threat to his own life the failure signified. At this moment he wrote that the Christian is the man who lives "unreservedly"!

Eberhard Bethge, Bonhoeffer's student and friend to whom most of the prison letters were addressed, remembered that while the young pastor was conducting a clandestine seminary in Nazi Germany, confronted constantly by threats to the closing of his theological classes, "he was unlikely to miss a bridge party."[10] Bonhoeffer was a man who lived joy in the midst of anxiety and death—without reservations.

The 21 July letter affirmed that by unreserved living "we throw ourselves completely into the arms of God, taking seriously, not our own sufferings, but those of God in the world—watching with Christ in Gethsemane. That, I think, is faith, that is *metanoia*; and that is how one becomes a man and a Christian." This puzzling sentence becomes meaningful when God is understood as the symbolic name for the impossible demands and absolute limits of life, which become *God* when a man "watches with Christ in Gethsemane."

Gethsemane, New Testament readers will remember, was the occasion upon which Jesus knew death to be near. He asked a few friends to be with him while he struggled with the crisis, the necessity of decision, facing him. The decision was whether he would attempt to avoid the death he saw coming or whether he would take it in stride. Jesus asked his friends to share with him the struggle of whether to fight against the goads or to receive the goads as his life definition.

The decision was, according to the story, far from easy (and many since have testified to the terror of the same decision necessity). Jesus' action was definitely open to his decision. No man struggles as the Gospel story has Jesus struggle if he knows already where he is to come out. Watching with Christ in Gethsemane is sharing the process of decision, making the decision for oneself. Jesus decided: if possible, I want to get out of this mess, but if not, let it come as the act of God, as the goodness of my life. And once the decision had been made, Jesus moved toward his end, taking all that came in stride. Jesus threw himself into the "arms of God." The disciples, however, refused to participate in the decision, a refusal they maintained until Pentecost.

The Secular Saint in the twentieth century knows the terrible isolation of living "completely in the arms of God." In earlier times, the arms of God could be understood as synonymous with the church or at least the groups of churchmen with whom a man lived and upon whom he depended. Today the Secular Saint has lost the security of living in a community, holy or otherwise. He now lives alone—even the family (the last vestige of community left to urban-secular man, and that only to middle- and upper-class existence) is no longer a secure refuge. The lives behind the statistics on divorce and broken homes testify to the fact that the home is a castle only so long as it performs a useful social function for those who constitute it. There may be real questions that the family has ever—save in isolated instances—matched the romantic vision that has been the hope of those who turned to it for final refuge from the isolation of contemporary existence.

Far from rejecting the family, the Secular Saint enjoys family relationships as much or more than any man. But he knows full well that the meaning of his life is not identical with those relationships. His life is secure even though his family disintegrates. His life is secure in his decision to trust his future to be good. His life is secure in the arms of God only, through his active decision (Holy Spirit) to embody the Christ possibility.

Causes and the Secular Saint

The Secular Saint gives his life to nothing but devotes his activity fully to specific endeavors. He resembles, but is infinitely different from, the American civil-rights worker who identifies himself entirely with "the movement." I have encountered such enthusiasts —white and Negro—who appear to be so identified with the Negro cause that, should their objectives be accomplished, their lives would become devoid of significance. Apart from the cause, they would not

exist. The Secular Saint knows such identity with specifics of existence to be nothing short of death. But he does not hesitate,
nevertheless, to become completely involved in specifics like the
Negro movement, living in the secure knowledge that they are not
his masters, that he is master of his involvement with them.

At the same time, the Secular Saint is under no obligation to
become related to or involved with movements or causes. He may
elect to isolate himself from these—and not necessarily in order to
become involved with something else. The Secular Saint refuses to
live by the law that says everyone must be involved with social movements. While he is defined by everything that is and transpires, he
is free to choose what he will devote his life to—and it may be simply
"the cleanliness of a washed pocket-handkerchief." The significant
matter is not the specific object of devotion, but the fact that the
Secular Saint chooses it, rather than falling unbeknownst into a
cause or routine or pattern of life.

The twentieth-century Secular Saint knows the isolation of working within mass movements—such as the Negro movement—that lay,
or attempt to lay, total claim on their adherents, for he refuses to
acquiesce to their ideology at the same time he fully supports their
social goals. He lives totally without defenses in society, including
the defenses provided by communities or groups of any kind. Trusting only in the security of the arms of God, the Secular Saint is able
to operate within mass movements, looking and acting—to an outside observer—like a total communicant. But the clue to his Sainthood is his willingness and his ability to drop the movement and
move on to other endeavors without guilt. In traditional religious
language, the Secular Saint refuses the lure of idolatry. No movement
and no charismatic person becomes the be-all and end-all of his life.
He is *self*-sufficient.

The Secular Saint is thus a definite threat to every mass movement, to every attempt to mold men into a preconceived life pattern.
He is a threat to all movements and causes that demand a stereotyped response to human and material conditions, including those
causes that bear a religious or Christian label. He affirms, instead,
the freedom to respond as he chooses and demands that freedom
for all others. In so doing, he affirms the freedom of other men to

choose the sin response to the limits and demands of their lives. Like Jesus with the rich young man, he twists no one's arm to get him to respond as he does. At the same time, he makes no bones about the claim of the Christ possibility as he receives it, and presents it to others as clearly as he can. At a different level, he exerts all the pressure at his command to achieve the social and political goals with which he has chosen to be associated. But, again, the achievement of those goals is not the rationale for his life, and their defeat or victory does not constitute the defeat or justification of his own being. He does what he can do and trusts the results into the arms of God.[11]

The Secular Saint lives, then, as an individual in the twentieth-century world. But since he remains aware of his socially constituted self, he is far from individualistic. Instead of isolating himself from the claims of other people and things as the individualist does, the Secular Saint keeps open every channel, admits every other. And instead of identifying himself with any movement or cause, he can work within every cause he chooses while combating the cause's absolute claim upon him and others.

The Secular Saint, therefore, is usually incomprehensible both to the individualist—the so-called rugged individualist—and to the fanatic of the mass movement. The individualist considers him a sell-out to the welfare state, the church, the civil-rights movement, or whatever. As such, the Secular Saint is rightly considered an enemy of the individualist's freedom to do what he "damn pleases." On the other hand, the fanatic is properly suspicious of the contemporary Saint, for the fanatic is extremely sensitive to deviation from the cause's "line," a deviation the Secular Saint embodies in his affirmation of himself as an individual. This twentieth-century Christian holds open the tension between giving his self away on either side—and he is fully aware that his is not a stance acceptable to the majority of those about him. But the Secular Saint receives the rejection of others, knowing painfully the pain, in the secure awareness of his life in the arms of God.

A *Life for Others*

No particular activity is distinctive to the Secular Saint. But the context in which he engages in any activity is distinctively his own. It is a context that conditions his activity, though in no wise determines it. I have suggested terminological ways of pointing to that context—freedom, selfhood, individual. But the context of Sainthood cannot be apprehended fully apart from the Secular Saint's direct responsibility toward the other selves that comprise his own selfhood. The Secular Saint wills the other who defines him to be a Secular Saint, too. He wills the other to live free, to be a dilettante, to be an individual. He wills the other to be a joyful self, receiving all that comprises his world as good, trusting only in the arms of God. In sum, the Secular Saint wills that the other embody the Christ possibility and reject the sin impossibility.

Why? Why should he be concerned for the way others respond to their lives (of which he is a part)? Granted, he has heard all his life that he is supposed to love other people, but now that he knows himself to be free from the law—even the law of love—why not let other people take care of themselves? The Secular Saint knows, when he reflects on the matter, that the question is already answered in his life-style. He knows he cannot be isolated from others, for his self is defined by those he would let alone. And he knows that their selves are defined in part by him; other selves are defined by their relationship matrix just as he is. A man has an impact on others whether he is a Secular Saint or not, but the Secular Saint chooses the character of that impact. He chooses to be the point at which the other is presented with the Christ possible response to life. He knows Martin Luther was right when he declared the faithful man to be Christ to his neighbor.

The Secular Saint is very clear: he does not talk *about* Christ to his neighbor; he *is* Christ to his neighbor, he *is* the "Word made flesh." The Secular Saint is the contemporary Jesus who presents his self as the Word of life to his neighbor; what he says and does and who he is are the same. Where he is, the possibility of receiving life as good is present, the possibility of living free is present, the necessity of fighting for life significance is revealed as being long gone. In sum, where he is Christ is, which is to say he *is* Christ. The Secular Saint is not Christ because he is some sort of special person; he is Christ because he has *chosen* to be Christ. He is not Christ because he has some sort of mystic insight; he is Christ because he has *chosen* to be Christ. He is not Christ because some far-off deity has sired him; he is Christ because in the Holy Spirit he has *chosen* to be Christ.[12]

The decision to be Christ—the specific historical embodiment of the real possibility for free, responsible, exciting living—is at the same time the decision to be a Secular Saint. That choice marks the difference between the licentious man and the Secular Saint, and between the Secular Saint and the legalist. The Secular Saint is everything the word Christ signifies; and Christ is everything connoted by the term Secular Saint. Herein lies the real significance of the ancient doctrine of the Incarnation. In Jesus of Nazareth the possibility of receiving all of life as a great, good gift was embodied: a man—Jesus—*was* that possibility.

But Jesus is no longer with us, and even if he were (if we lived when Jesus lived, so to speak) the possibility that he was is meaningless unless it is a genuine possibility for you and me. Possibilities must be accepted or chosen if they are to be meaningful. They certainly are not built in. No man can be Christ, or a Secular Saint, unless he *chooses* Christ as the operating mode of his life.

When I say that the Secular Saint is the point at which others encounter the Christ possibility, I do not mean that any particular Secular Saint is the only Christ embodiment. Far from it. Any and every man may be Christ—and the Secular Saint longs for the day (the end of the world? the eschaton?) when all men will embody the Christ possibility. His problem is not to coerce others into being Christ; his problem is to be Christ himself, to choose constantly to be Christ. The response of others is their problem.

Like Jesus of Nazareth, the Secular Saint may be called names. Pious folk call him blasphemous or arrogant. Nonreligious men think him ridiculous, like a grown man seriously wearing a Superman suit. But as we have seen, the Secular Saint does not conduct himself on the basis of such judgments. He lives free—free to say yes when he chooses to say yes, free to say no when he chooses to say no, free to obey or not obey the dictates of those about him. He is free to choose to be Christ to his fellows. In his freedom the Secular Saint allows every other to lay his claim upon him, to which he responds with a demonstration of the reception of life as good, offering that response as a live option for the other's choosing. But how does a man do that?

The classic New Testament demonstration of the Christ presentation is Jesus' story about the Samaritan who assisted a hapless robbery victim. Telling the story in response to the direct question, "Who is my neighbor?", he typically answered with an anecdote, not an abstract description, that left it up to his interrogator to determine for himself whether the priest or the Levite or the Samaritan *acted* the part of the neighbor. Today the question (since the word neighbor is virtually useless in our urban society) is "How may I be Christ?" or "How may I make the Christ possibility available?"

We already know the answer, just as Jesus' contemporaries knew the answer to their question. After all, the Gospel story gives evidence that the priest and the Levite knew the man in the ditch was laying a claim upon them. Twentieth-century men have little difficulty identifying with these ancient ecclesiastical authorities. We, too, have diverse claims upon our time, energy, and resources. We, too, must make decisions about priorities. We, too, must assume the guilt for our failure to be Christ at one point when we choose to affirm other pressing claims. Jesus' story, significantly, makes no necessary judgment on the priest and the Levite, but simply asked after their response to the man in the ditch. He did not inquire similarly about their other self relationships.

Today's Secular Saint takes the necessity of a complex existence fully into account. He sits loose to the demands of his own "man in the ditch"—but he also sits loose to the demands of his organizational existence. Knowing that his life does not finally depend upon the approval of his wife or his boss, he can freely decide when and where he will spend his time and money.

In the manner of Jesus, let us say that Henry, a typical organization man, learns, before leaving for work in the morning, that a casual acquaintance has been arrested for homosexual activities and he needs someone to bail him out of jail. If help does not come immediately, he will be jailed for the day or even longer.

At his office, Henry has a long-scheduled meeting with his superiors to discuss the possibility of appointment to a position from which he may influence many others in their future development. A vice-president from another city will be present to make the decision. The appointment depends upon Henry's presence and his presentation.

As a Secular Saint, Henry quickly weighs the alternatives. If he helps his friend, he will miss the vice-president and, probably, the chance for the new position. If he goes on to the office, he may get the position and the extra opportunity for wider service, but a man who needs help may end up in jail. As the contemporary Christ, what must he do?

Literal readers of the New Testament would assure him that he must help the arrested man. Moralists would tell him that the man deserves everything he will get; Henry should go to the office. Henry's own inclination is to make his meeting; he wants the job and knows he can be Christ to many people he would otherwise not touch through it. He is fully aware that his friends would probably approve his inclination, but he knows also that the man arrested for homosexual activities needs his help.

Henry, as a Secular Saint, takes all these considerations seriously but none are capable of making his decision for him. He cannot go to the meeting with the company officials *because* the incarcerated man is immoral or *because* he thinks the greater number of people would be served as a result of his presence in the new position. On the other hand, he cannot rush down to the police station *because* a man has a problem and asked him for help. Neither can he do so *because* he does not want to and thus would feel guilty if he did not. Henry must make a free decision; there are no rules to decide for him.

Clearly, freedom is not the most happy context for Henry. But then no one ever said Christian faith was easy; in fact, the New Testament makes it clear that the "burden is heavy" and the "road is narrow." Let us shoot this script both ways.

(1) Henry decides to tell the accused homosexual that his busi-

ness is so pressing he cannot come post bail. The man declares that he knows nowhere else to turn and that if Henry refuses to come he will be unable to get out in time to find the only witness who could clear him. Even so, Henry tells him, he cannot come; he'll see him that evening. But the evening will be too late, comes the reply. Sorry, says Henry, and hangs up.

On the way to his office Henry turns on the radio, listens to the news, the weather, and a couple of songs plus commercials. He wonders what will happen to the man he decided not to help, but he is most concerned with how he will make his case for the program he would implement in the new job that is open. Finally, he turns off the radio in order to be certain of missing none of the thoughts that crowd their way into his mind. The decision about the accused homosexual is a thing of the past.

(2) Henry calls his office and tells his secretary he will be late and cannot make the scheduled meeting. He asks her to convey his regrets to the vice-president, hangs up the telephone, dashes to his automobile and drives toward the police station after stopping at the bank's drive-in window to cash a check for the bail money.

As he drives, Henry finds himself hoping the vice-president will be able to stay until afternoon, but then the image of his friend shoves its way to the fore. Can he help him find the witness after the bail is posted? Is he helping a *real* homosexual? Does it make any difference? Henry has made his decision about the office meeting; the problem is now at the precinct station.

The point here is that the Secular Saint is absolutely free to decide as he chooses to decide, and to implement his decision without regret because he did not choose otherwise. He knows the rules and the mores of his culture but he lives free of them, preferring to make his own decisions and take the full consequences of them, for only in that way is he truly free.

But how is he demonstrating the Christ possibility to anyone by either decision? Certainly he is not going to outline his decision-making process either to the arrested man or to the vice-president. Once more, let's shoot the scene both ways.

(1) Arriving at his office just in time for the meeting, Henry collects his material and enters the meeting room. The vice-president

and his immediate superior are already seated. Henry outlines his plan for the future as completely as he can and waits for the reaction. The vice-president is impressed by the plan, but he is particularly impressed by Henry's calm and relaxed, though competent, manner. He asks Henry to have lunch with him.

Over lunch, the vice-president comments on Henry's presentation, particularly upon his apparent assurance. How, he wants to know, is Henry able to be so confident in what is normally a tense situation? Whereupon, Henry tells him that, in the first place, he thinks his plan is a good one. In the second place, he knows that, while the plan and the job are important, his whole life does not hinge on them, and that, therefore, he need not be anxious about success or failure at that point. He suggests to the vice-president that nothing is so important that its failure can deprive him of an exciting life. And, incidentally, the vice-president's life is significant, too; he doesn't need to be threatened by his job either.

Does Henry get the job? We won't take the scene that far. Perhaps he does. Perhaps he makes the vice-president angry at lunch and the job goes to someone else. But in either case, the vice-president has encountered a free man—a Secular Saint—whose freedom presents the possibility of freedom even for a vice-president. Life is good if he chooses it to be good.

(2) Upon arrival at the police station, Henry hands over the required money and the released man then accompanies him out to the car. Henry wants to know if he can take him anywhere, but the accused homosexual can hardly answer, so angry is he at his treatment by the police. They had no right to pick him up in the first place or to book him in the second. Homosexual acts between consenting adults should not be an offense anyway. That may be, Henry says, but the law is the law and you can hardly blame the police for enforcing it.

The man tells Henry that he is in fact a homosexual but that he was not engaged in a criminal act when arrested this time. He is actually innocent of the specific charge. Henry is not sure whether he can believe his companion or not, but that is not his problem anyway. After all, Henry is neither a judge nor a jury. He is only a man who posted bail and offered a ride.

As they proceed toward the address where the witness lives, the man suddenly turns to Henry and wonders how Henry can get away from his job all this time. Henry tells him that he just didn't go to work that day and that it's nothing to worry about. Let's just hope the witness is still here. The man begins to speculate on what will happen to him if he cannot prove he is innocent. His whole life will be ruined, he is certain. To which Henry suggests that it may not be as bad as all that; even conviction on a morals charge cannot take away his significance. He is, Henry tells him, an important person no matter what—if he chooses to be.

That's absurd, the man tells Henry. Be that as it may, Henry replies, but it's still true. About this time, Henry stops the car at the address given him and they walk to the door and knock.

Whether the witness is there and whether the accused homosexual is found innocent shall be left unknown. What is important for our purposes is that the man was confronted with a Secular Saint who demonstrated the goodness of life and offered the same possibility to him. Whether he receives it or not, the accused man has encountered the possibility of freedom, he has bumped into Christ.

Henry's situation and the complexities of his decision necessity could of course have taken a number of turns other than the ones outlined above. But the style of the Secular Saint would have been, in whatever case, to make his own free decision about his own life and to embody the possibility of life's goodness in the process. The Secular Saint must choose over and over again to be Christ, never knowing the final result of his embodiment of the Christ possibility. It is interesting to note that Jesus, Peter, and Paul never counseled with people. They made Christ available in such fashion that the hearer was forced to say yes or no. The question of how the Secular Saint is to demonstrate the Christ possibility does not ask for a method of communication. The Secular Saint's problem is not how to "communicate the gospel"; his problem is how to be Christ. The two are not the same.

An ancient story has Moses out on a mountain tending his father-in-law's sheep.[13] Noticing a bush on fire but not burning up, Moses goes to check it out and discovers himself to be confronted with

God as a demand to lead the people of Israel out of Egypt. Moses is not too excited at the prospect and tries to get out of the job, but God insists, suggesting some techniques that should be effective in securing the people's release. Still Moses is reluctant: "I am not eloquent . . . but am slow of speech and of tongue." Today he might say that he didn't have the proper communication training, or that he didn't know the right vocabulary, or hadn't been to seminary, or needed knowledge of group dynamics.

According to the story, God dismisses the communication argument as irrelevant: "Who has made man's mouth? Who makes him dumb, or deaf, or seeing, or blind? Is it not I, the Lord? Now therefore go, and I will be with your mouth and teach you what you shall speak." Decide to take this job, God was saying, and the ways to get it done will come along—and so they do, when Moses keeps insisting he cannot do it. Let Aaron talk then, God says, but you've got to be responsible for what he says. Finally, Moses has to decide to go get the people out, and that is all the equipment he needs at the time. He can find the proper tools when they become necessary.

The Secular Saint has made the decision to be Christ (the point at which the real possibility of living without the support of laws and approval becomes available) to those about him. And when he hesitates, claiming inadequate preparation, he is simply trying to dodge the issue, refusing to follow through on his decision. Before the Christ possible response to life, nothing is required save the decision to receive it as one's own. It is a decision for Christ (life) or sin (death). The living out of the Holy Spirit life is a pragmatic problem that cannot be tackled outside of or prior to the Christ decision. Being Christ is not a communication problem.

Our day has become obsessed with the idea of communication. Churches, no less than the communication media, are deeply engaged with the discovery of the most efficient devices for transmitting a message from one individual or group to another. Assumed throughout is that something is present to communicate. I am reminded of the free-speech advocates who, upon achieving their objective, find they don't know what to say. The gospel, the good news of the possibility for life affirmation, is not a package to be distributed, like a brand of cigarettes. The Secular Saint finds him-

WITHDRAWN FROM THE MILWAUKEE PUBLIC LIBRARY NOT FOR RESALE

self sadly laughing at efforts to market Christian faith through jingles on radio and television. On the other hand, he trusts God sufficiently not to be trapped in the faithless act of concern for the words he is to say or how or when he is to say them. He *is* the Word. The words come when he launches out as the Christ.

The Secular Saint is under no illusion as to the efficiency of his Christ embodiment. He is fully aware that there is no way to test immediately (or perhaps even in the long run) whether or not the possibility he embodies has been received. He even has no assurance that, in his effort to make Christ available, he has not presented a new and even more demonic form of bondage—and he doesn't care.

Before someone shouts that this Secular Saint is callous and cruel, really unconcerned for what he does to others, let me make clear that the Secular Saint's not caring whether he leads men to life or death has nothing to do with his desire that all those who comprise the definition of his self (and we know by now that that is all-inclusive) live as free men. He knows, though, that whether the other lives or dies is the decision of the other; the Secular Saint himself has no control over the decision. The other is free, and the Secular Saint would be the last to try relieving him of his freedom, even though his free choice is for sin and death.

Once again, the Secular Saint stands outside of all mass movements, which always try to brainwash men so they will be "free" to choose only the stance of the movement. He is, nevertheless, particularly vulnerable to religious mass movements of a creative and Christ-centered type. These hold great fascination for the Secular Saint, for they proclaim the gospel of Jesus Christ—but in such a way as to place the sin response outside the realm of possibility. Any movement—no matter how Christian it may be—that would deny sin's practical possibility is fundamentally rejected by the Secular Saint, who insists on radical freedom. Bear in mind that the Secular Saint is not happy when men choose death, but he doesn't run after them to twist their arms to adopt the Christ response to life. His job is finished when he offers, as a live option, the possibility of trusting the absolute limits and impossible demands of life to be very good. The response is the arms of God.

The alternative to not caring about the other's response to the

Christ possibility is allowing the response of the other to justify the Secular Saint's action and life. But the Secular Saint is not justified —made right or good—by anything, including the favorable response by an other to his embodiment of Christ. What he does not care about, finally, is any effort to maintain his self; his self is always already secure. Therefore, he is totally free to be concerned for the other in the hope that the other may clearly understand the wonderful life possibility standing before him in the person of Christ.

From the perspective of the Secular Saint, it becomes possible for contemporary men to understand what the spokesmen for the church have meant when they spoke of selflessness. They certainly have not meant some kind of disinterest in the self. When that meaning has been implied by selflessness, a horrible form of pride has lurked close beneath the surface. The man who pretends to himself and others that he is not interested in his self only hides the fact that his un-self-ishness is his way of trying to maintain his self in the image he finds most attractive. The Secular Saint, on the other hand, is intensely interested in his self, and for that very reason lives for others, desiring them to receive their selves as always already secure, too.

Among the terms left ambiguous by Bonhoeffer's prison letters is "transcendence."[14] In his outline for a book, Bonhoeffer promised to discuss later "the experience that a transformation of all human life is given in the fact that 'Jesus is there only for others'. His 'being there for others' is the experience of transcendence."[15] I have the strong suspicion that transcendence points in the direction of the Secular Saint's confidence in his already secure selfhood. What is transcended is any necessity to secure or protect the self—which becomes clearly evident in the Secular Saint's activity "for others." Jesus, the prototype of the Secular Saint, exemplifies *par excellence* the transcendent life. "It is only this 'being there for others', maintained till death," Bonhoeffer wrote, "that is the ground of [Jesus'] omnipotence, omniscience, and omnipresence. Faith is participation in this being of Jesus (incarnation, cross, and resurrection). Our relation to God is not a 'religious' relationship to the highest, most powerful, and best Being imaginable—that is not authentic transcendence—but our relation to God is a new life in 'existence for others', through participation in the being of Jesus. The transcendental is not infinite and unattainable tasks, but the neighbor who is within reach in any given situation. God in human form— not, as in oriental religions, in animal form, monstrous, chaotic, remote, and terrifying, nor in the conceptual forms of the absolute, metaphysical, infinite, etc., nor yet in the Greek divine-human form of 'man in himself', but 'the man for others', and therefore the Crucified, the man who lives out of the transcendent."[16] Jesus, as the Secular Saint, lived for others as transcendent, because that is exactly what it means to be infinitely concerned for self.

Before leaving this passage in the prison letters, I cannot fail to observe further the sentence: "The transcendental is not infinite and unattainable tasks, but the neighbor who is within reach in any given situation." The Secular Saint knows his life is not, and never will be, lived in some far-distant realm. It is lived, and always will be, with "the neighbor who is within reach," where the definition of his self is immediately presented to him. His life is received as constantly presented with the necessity to choose freedom, joy, hope, pleasure, suffering, labor, as good *or* as bad. His choice becomes concrete in his action toward "the neighbor who is within reach." In the 1960's, it must be noted, the thing within reach often includes events transpiring halfway around the world; no man today can avoid reading, hearing, and even seeing these formerly distant and unknown happenings. The whole world has come into his living room. When his own life is received as good and secure, the Secular Saint is indeed free to be the man for others.

Does the Secular Saint exist? Do men who live the life of Secular Sainthood actually move on the earth? I am constantly surprised that this question inevitably arises when I discuss the Secular Saint in private conversation. The question stems from a fundamental skepticism that any man can live free, receiving all that comes as good and for his good, always offering the possibility of that life to others. The question, in other words, is still the rich young man's. And the answer must be the answer the young man received: try it and see.

6

Saints Together

There was a man with tongue of wood
Who essayed to sing,
And in truth it was lamentable.
But there was one who heard
The clip-clapper of this tongue of wood
And knew what the man
Wished to sing,
And with that the singer was content.

Stephen Crane

WHAT HAPPENS when Secular Saints get together? Or do they get together? As an individual, why would the Secular Saint want to get together with other Secular Saints—or anyone else, for that matter?

Questions such as these inevitably arise when the Secular Saint is talked about (instead of simply lived). They arise principally because men still live in fear of isolation, but with a romantic attraction to rugged individualism. Both togetherness and lonely omnipotence have their appeal. Coupled with these is the tenacious refusal to receive the Christ possibility, the refusal to stand radically open to life, receiving all that comes as good. Apart from the Christ possibility, enacted through the Holy Spirit as the Secular Saint, the radically free existence discussed in Chapter 5 would be demonic rejection of life, an effort to cut oneself off from the world about. But, as we have seen, the Secular Saint, far from rejecting the others about him, actively wills his relationship with them. Particularly, he desires fellowship with other Secular Saints, but is under no illusion that they are more likable than other people.

Once the Secular Saint has chosen to be Christ to his neighbor, and has embarked on his mission of being the point at which others encounter the possibility of choosing free and accountable living, he quickly discovers that he cannot be Christ to himself. "The Christ in his own heart is weaker than the Christ in the word of his brother; his own heart is uncertain, his brother's is sure."[1] Memory, valuable and necessary as it is, is notoriously fickle; it has the nasty habit of bringing to consciousness only those events and decisions that justify self-denial or sin. The Word in Jesus Christ stands always external to the man who has chosen to be Christ. Perhaps the uniqueness of the Christ embodiment by Jesus of Nazareth lies in his total aloneness. The disciples did not and could not offer the life possibility he required, as their sleep while Jesus wrestled with the decision about his response to impending death gives evidence. But the historical testimony in the scriptures remained with him in memory. At this point, also, the uniqueness of this man comes through: his historical memory was not buttressed by testimony from others living within his immediate self. The Secular Saint is not Jesus of Nazareth; the Christ in his heart is still uncertain, requiring the Christ Word from his brother, traditionally through the church.

When we reflect on the historical images of the church, three come immediately to mind: body of Christ, people of God, and communion of Saints.

The Body of Christ

The body of Christ image makes genuine sense to the Secular Saint, for the body of Christ points toward the embodiment of the Christ possibility he has chosen as his life mode or Lord. The body of Christ may be understood in at least two ways by contemporary man. In the first place, it suggests the Secular Saint himself. It means, quite literally, the *body* of Christ, in this case the body of the Secular Saint. It means the physical presence of the Christ Word operating in contemporary history. The Secular Saint, under this image, is the body of Christ; his presence is the presence of the Christ possibility. The body of Christ equals the Secular Saint.

In the second place, the body of Christ may be understood as the body "having many members," each with its particular function. This image, too, makes sense to the Secular Saint. No particular Secular Saint is able to speak the necessary Word to every part of his definition. Because he is an individual, with individual gifts and inclinations, he cannot touch directly every other individual within his self. And, among those he can touch, he is not always the most strategic person to declare the Word directly. Every Secular Saint requires other Secular Saints in order to make the freeing declaration to his self-defined world. The body of Christ has indeed many members.

In both understandings of the body of Christ, the Secular Saint remains the free, accountable individual. In the first instance, he is the complete embodiment of the Christ possibility. The Secular Saint *is* the Christ to his neighbor, he *is* the body of Christ. But it is not always strategic for the Secular Saint overtly to declare the Word (another may do it more effectively). He is a *member* of the body of Christ. Both understandings of the body of Christ make sense to the contemporary man of Christian faith.

The People of God

The people of God is another matter. The Secular Saint has more difficulty with this one; for the people of God bears an exclusive and communal freight that is not consistent with the free life of the Secular Saint.

A story is told of an American oil company that found one of its jeeps missing. A check of its employees showed no misuse of company property. The jeep had been stolen. The vehicle was finally traced to a particular Arab tribe, but when company officials interrogated tribal officers and members, the same answer was forthcoming: "I stole it." Each member of the tribe assumed responsibility for the theft of the automobile, which was resting in the center of the nomadic encampment. All efforts by the company to assess individual guilt met with frustration. The *tribe* stole the jeep. Finally, the company representatives took the jeep and went home. After they had left, the tribe gathered, determined who had taken the car (thus jeopardizing the position of the tribe relative to the oil company), and punished him according to tribal custom.

The Arab tribe demonstrates the context in which the people of God image is relevant. As was often the case with primitive peoples, the tribe or community or family defined the individual. Without the tribe the individual did not exist; individual and communal action were identical. Such was the social context in which the Old Testament literature developed. It would scarcely have made sense to Old Testament thought patterns to speak of a man of faith; men were not faithful, people were. In a few Old Testament writings, the individual element did begin to develop, especially Job and Ezekiel. While the great prophets spoke as separate individuals, they did not address themselves to individuals, nor call individuals to repentance—they called Israel, the People of God, back to the covenant relationship with God.

Twentieth-century men have a difficult time comprehending the significance of the tribe for the life of individual man, but tribal men would have an equally difficult time comprehending the present-day understanding of the individual apart from the community. Of modern images, the larger family and the nation come closest to the ancient tribe (still present in some parts of Africa, Latin America, and Asia).

The larger family is the tribe in miniature. Normally, it is comprised of parents, grandparents, uncles, aunts, and cousins, all of whom live within a limited geographical area that allows frequent contact among family units and individuals within the families. Usually, the men are engaged in similar remunerative activity, such as farming, and the women and children are supportive of that activity. While the center of authority does not rest on a single person (in the tribe, the chief, who is the principal embodiment of the tribe itself), the grandfather or patriarch exercises considerable influence until he becomes senile.

As a young pastor, I once served a church in an isolated rural area that was rapidly being bypassed by civilization—the main highway had been built elsewhere and the land was not producing as it once had. The principal problem of the community, I was told, was that the young people were all leaving for the cities, becoming educated and taking jobs hundreds and thousands of miles away; few people were left to work the farms. The center of the community was the church, which, I was told, used to be filled each Sunday morning and Wednesday night and had overflowed during the annual week-long revival. But now only a handful of elderly parents and grandparents remained to huddle around the oilstove on Sunday mornings, the Wednesday night prayer meeting was long gone, and the big event of the year was the church "homecoming," during which a popular former pastor was invited to preach and for which the far-flung children and grandchildren were urged, often unsuccessfully, to return.

The problem, so those who remained told me, was the lure of the city. But, whatever the cause, the real difficulty was the breakup of the larger family. No longer were mature children making decisions in the same way their fathers had made them. No longer did the community of relations determine what they did and who they were. And, significantly, no longer were the religious beliefs and practices of the community determinative for them. Many in the younger generation didn't even belong to the denomination of their parents, and some, the shame of the larger family, professed no religious belief at all. This younger generation, some of whom were well into middle age, had chosen to live as it wished, and knew no guilt or deprivation by virtue of leaving the larger family, a development that those whose lives were lived and determined by the family could neither understand nor forgive.

Like the tribe, the larger family could speak of the people of God, for the larger family was a *people*, a community tied together by blood, tradition, custom, and history. A young man lived out his life under the aegis of his father's God, who became his God in turn, to be passed on to his children. Not only was God the God of the family, but the family was the people of God. In a meaningful sense, the Old Testament covenant, "I will be your God and you will be my people," was the covenant of the larger family that existed well into the twentieth century as a primary model for family and community self-understanding.

The nation is the tribe writ large. The modern nation particularly has tried to perform the function of the ancient close-knit community. And just as the larger family lived with its version of the Old Testament covenant, so has the modern nation. Perhaps the most vivid example was Germany during the 1930's and 1940's, where the individual clearly was supposed to derive his significance from the nation. Good and morality were defined by the best interests of the nation, as Adolf Hitler repeatedly made clear. In this case, the nation began to assume the role of God, true, but it was also a context in which an external God played a vital supportive role. God was the God of the German state and the German state was the people of God, who had set this people apart from all other peoples on earth.

Like the tribe, Hitler's Germany understood itself in terms of its heroic and romantic past (a good bit of which had to be manufactured for the occasion). The people were one people in blood, tradition, and glorious future. But Hitler was finally unable to bring off his modern supertribe.

The tribal elements of the nation, however, have remained with contemporary civilization, and they become no more evident than in the supernationalism that would divide the world into East and West. In both the United States and the Soviet Union, the language of religion is seldom invoked. In its stead, powerful verbal symbols have arisen in such words as "democracy" and "freedom," words that take the role formerly played by "God." The covenant still reads, "I will be your God and you will be my People," but "democracy" or "freedom" is the speaker, instead of the great old God of the mountain, Yahweh, or his gentle Incarnation, Jesus of Nazareth. The nation, so many believe, cannot be the nation unless it is simultaneously a *community*, bound together by common blood and history, the latter to be made by shedding the former.

It is a truism that dangers from an external source weld people together. As long as men have an enemy in common they are able to sidetrack or ignore their otherwise divisive individuality. Thus, in the United States communism becomes the enemy, as capitalism is the enemy in Russia. In each case, the enemy must be defeated at all costs—except the greatest cost of all to a modern nation: loss of its communal identity, or, in other words, its national sovereignty.

The people of God image does not create the larger family or the modern nation, but these are contexts in which that image can emerge. Like the family and the nation, the people of God is an exclusive and communal image—it requires those who are *not* people of God, who must either be incorporated (converted) or destroyed (damned).

The Secular Saint does not seek out the people of God, for he knows his life and mission is not the life and mission of the church, much less of the larger family or the nation. His life is his own to choose entirely as he wills under the symbol of the Christ possibility. The life of the Secular Saint, therefore, is significantly different from that of the churchman, who is defined by the church as the people of God. The individual churchman is the embodiment of the church, he carries with him the entire community throughout history. When he speaks, the church speaks, the people of God (as distinct from those who are not the people of God) speaks.

The radical character of the New Testament lies in its broadening of the people of God concept to the point where it loses its exclusive and communal content. Jesus is pictured as healing those who are not Jews (the People of God) as well as those who are. Of particular note is the healing of the Syrophoenician woman's daughter: "Then Jesus left and went away to the territory near the city of Tyre. He went into a house and did not want anyone to know he was there, but he could not stay hidden. A certain woman, whose daughter had an evil spirit in her, heard about Jesus and came to him at once and fell at his feet. The woman was a foreigner, born in Phoenicia of Syria. She begged Jesus to drive the demon out of her daughter. But Jesus answered, 'Let us feed the children first; it isn't right to take the children's food and throw it to the dogs.' 'Sir,' she answered, 'even the dogs under the table eat the children's leftovers!' So Jesus said to her, 'For such an answer you may go home; the demon has gone out of your daughter!' So she went back home and there found her child lying on the bed; the demon had indeed gone out of her."[2]

Obviously, it was not easy for Jesus to break through the tribal understanding of the chosen people, but break through he did. Those who came after completed the broadening of the people image. The people of God no longer could serve as a normative image for those who had responded to the Christ possibility, which is available to all who have ears to hear.[3]

Paul put the finishing touches on the destruction of any exclusionism for the followers of Christ. The Christ possibility, Paul declared, was for "the Jew first, but also for the Greek."[4] Further, "through faith you are all sons of God in union with Christ Jesus baptized into the union with him, you have all put on Christ as a garment, there is no such thing as Jew and Greek, slave and freeman, male and female; for you are all one person in Christ Jesus."[5]

It is clear that Paul did not reject the people of God image, but his formulation for it was radically different. Instead of a foundation in the community, with its traditions and regulations, the people of God was now founded on faith: "through *faith* you are all sons of God." In other words, a "son of God" is born when a man chooses Christ as his Lord, thus making the Christ response to the limiting and demanding activity of his self the operating mode of his life.

When the definition of a term has been as radically altered as the New Testament altered "the people of God," there is real question as to the term's usefulness. It is not surprising, therefore, that another image arose for the church, incorporating oneness in Christ, which has an affinity with "the people of God" while maintaining the individuality of the lonely decision for the Christ possibility demanded of all who have ears to hear. That image is the communion of Saints.

The Communion of Saints

The communion of Saints is the people of God upside down. Whereas under the image of the people of God the individual is the locus of the community, in which genuine reality resides, under the communion of Saints image the community is the locus of the individual. The Secular Saint rejects the people of God as a model for his own existence. He knows that Paul was right to make trust in what comes to him in his life normative for the church. He knows "salvation is through the church" only when the church is understood as the communion of Saints; when the church is the people of God the individual member loses his right to make free decisions relative to Christ and sin.

The communion of Saints is congregational, not communal. The distinction is crucial, for twentieth-century men do not live in communities. Efforts to develop communities are successful to the extent that they isolate community members from other persons, if not by space and time, by ideology. Any community in the twentieth century exists as an identifiable enclave among those who live in no community. Exciting and creative as they may be, communal structures do not jibe with twentieth-century life. Now is the day of the Secular Saint.

Because he can no longer understand himself as the embodiment of a particular community, the Secular Saint is left with the problem of the particular type of multiself associations in which he finds himself. The image of the communion of Saints seems ready-made for him, for it is an individual image, an image that holds at its center the Secular Saint who makes his own free decisions without support of men, circumstances, or principles, including communities, larger families, tribes, or nations.

The Congregation of Saints

The communion of Saints is the conscious interrelationship of Secular Saints. Nothing holds them together—no tradition, history, law, custom, or ideology—except the fact that each has responded affirmatively to the Christ possibility. Nothing else is requisite for membership in the communion of Saints. The communion of Saints is defined only by Christ. "Jesus Christ in the midst of his people who are gathered in his name (Matthew 18:20) is a *complete* definition of the church. He who wants more than this ends up with less."[6] When two or three are gathered, there is Christ in the midst of them, or, more contemporary, when Christ is present two or three become aware of it—and of each other. Once again, those who become aware of Christ in their midst may have nothing else in common. But Christ is enough. At that moment, the Saints have congregated.

Being in the communion of Saints is not the same, however, as being in the congregation of Saints. When a man enters the former he enters into communion with all others who have made the decision for the Christ possibility; he "tunes in on the same channel" as have countless others in the past and as will countless others in the future—that he may never encounter them personally is not important. The congregation of Saints, on the other hand, is the physical presence of two or more Secular Saints to each other, which event has sometimes been called the "gathered church." No special importance is attached to this congregation, nothing hangs on it; its participants remain within the communion of Saints whether they congregate or not.

Nevertheless, the congregation is of signal pragmatic importance, for in this congregation the Secular Saint is constantly confronted anew with his obligation to reduplicate the Holy Spirit decision in concrete action—and fulfills his obligation to so confront his companions in Sainthood.

What do Secular Saints do when they congregate? They worship and they study.

The Worship Party

Formal worship often is a genuine problem for the Secular Saint, because it is so closely tied to the religion he must reject. He knows that the need for celebration at the Christ possibility is constantly with him, but only in very special instances is what passes for worship in the churches any kind of celebration. Once that has been said, however, I must hasten to note that Secular Saints are the most likely people to participate in traditional worship with genuine joy; God, Christ, and the Holy Spirit are the style of their living. Nevertheless, they find worship—genuine celebration—to be an association with others that transpires far more frequently and in much less structural form than the traditional gatherings in church buildings on Sunday morning.

Any congregation of Secular Saints, even conversation between two in casual encounter, is celebration, is worship, but the semiformal congregation develops its own worship patterns, one of which may take the form of a party, not just any party, but a celebration of the Christ possibility and its reception in the Holy Spirit. During the summer of 1966, the Faith and Culture Institute (Washington, D.C.) conducted a series of studies in experimental theology with participants in a project called Students in Urban Affairs, sponsored by the General Board of Christian Social Concerns of The Methodist Church and the Methodist Student Movement. The summer's experiment included free-floating worship that eventuated in a worship party, which had many of the formal characteristics of a child's birthday party. Looking back, I can see a form of worship that could make real sense to many congregations of Saints.

A child's birthday party moves through a rather definite ritual that includes the greeting of guests, the giving and receiving of gifts, games (usually organized by the birthday child's mother), a ceremonial meal, with favors for the guests and a candle-laden cake, highlighted by the blowing out of the candles. The purpose is to declare the significance of the child's progress toward adulthood. The outline of the ritual is fairly stable, at least in middle-class American culture.

The purpose of the Secular Saints' worship is to celebrate the great, good gift of the Christ possible response to life and the free life that results from the Holy Spirit decision to receive that gift. Worship is the celebration of the Christ in the midst—and what a celebration it is! For too long, worship services have been solemn affairs that people have attended through some sense of duty. Such services are a mockery of worship; they deny the central *raison d'être* for the celebration, which is joy in the free life of the Holy Spirit, joy in the gift of the Christ possibility, joy in the claim and limit of God. For the Secular Saint, worship is celebration.

As in other types of celebration, the worship of the congregation of Saints includes a recital of the reason for celebration, including recognition of the conditions that prevailed prior to the celebrated event. Such recital is the "first act" of the celebration: confession and absolution. Renouncing confession as a catalogue of moral violations, the Secular Saint and his fellows confess or admit or recognize themselves to be the people they actually are. In so doing, they remember that they are defined in terms of the complex relationship matrices that are their selves, that they have repeatedly chosen not be the selves they are but have elected the sin response toward the absolute limits and impossible demands of their lives; that they have chosen not to be free, decisive men and women.

Confession is properly a rather sober, reflective affair, a mood that does not jibe with the usual image of a party or celebration. But a worship party is not a normal party—it is a particular kind of party that adheres to its own dynamic, the dynamic of the Christian faith. Thus, the beginning of the worship party may well belie the merrymaking that is to follow.

The somber mood of confession is requisite to the subsequent whoopee, for Secular Saints know the whoopee is occasioned by the liberating Word that can be proclaimed only as they are loosed from the bondage of self-denial. It is important to note that Secular

Saints have already heard the Christ possibility and received it as the operating mode of their lives. When they confess, they confess that they have not reduplicated that reception in concrete living. Had they not made the decision for Christ, their self-denial would be made conscious in the Christ Word itself, but at this late stage in faithfulness they find it necessary to separate their refusal to live as they have chosen to live from the renewed possibility of saying yes to life that comes again as the Christ. Nobody becomes a Secular Saint for life; each man must remake the decision for Christ again and again.

Recognition of the sobriety of confession in no way denies or denigrates the vivacity of the entire worship party. For the Saints together, confession may well be one with absolution. In the traditional worship service of the Christian church, confession, the recognition that "we have done those things that we ought not to have done, and we have left undone those things that we ought to have done," is followed by words of absolution in which the possibility of receiving the Christ possibility is offered afresh. But this careful sequential distinction between confession and absolution is not absolutely necessary for the Secular Saints together, particularly if the party participants engage in no organized corporate activity. The conversation that develops will center on the experiences of the individuals present that have revealed to them their refusal to receive life as for their good—and the absolution is present in the response of the hearers, who remind those present that, no matter what the past, the future is open. Confession, in other words, takes place within the *context* of the Christ possibility.

"All silly stateliness and all hocus-pocus, which so often spoil our church life, can be forgotten, yes, *must* be left behind in such groups, for it just does not fit in.

Now everyone gets a chance to remove his mask and to bring up the questions that really concern him. What are those? In general, it seems to me, they are not the questions of guilt and forgiveness, which are so central in the church's proclamation. It is rather the question whether human existence is still livable. To put it quite primitively: Can one still be a Christian and at the same time be fully a modern person? And how?"[7]

It may well be that the refreshments are not made available at the worship party until the Secular Saints have had the opportunity to engage in the confession-absolution conversation. After the guests have arrived and entered into conversation with each other, the host of the evening makes the goodies available. This action signals a progression in the worship party similar to the ringing of the bell and/or the saying of the versicle in the age-old worship of Christians. It is the signal for the jubilation in the reception of the Christ possibility to commence, the beginning of Act II: praise and adoration.

The majority of the worship party's space and time is spent in Act II. The Secular Saints simply have a good time, doing what anyone else does at a party—talking, singing, dancing. No particular content to the talk and movement is prescribed; the guests simply revel in their fellowship, but none may escape the awareness that theirs is profound "joy in the Lord." Finally, the celebration is celebration of the Christ possibility, reception of which has released them to participate fully in everything presented by the life that is theirs.

The Secular Saints together are in intimate danger, of course, of the pitfall into which Paul accused the Christians at Corinth of falling.[8] Their celebration may well turn totally toward self-denial, or the delusion that they are not responsible for their relationships with all other persons and things, that they may do as they please without consequence to themselves or others. But, once more, that is a danger they willingly face—always ready to be called back by the Paul in their midst.

The host of the worship party remains acutely aware of the worship character of the event. He is careful to recognize that Act II is not the totality of the celebration. Unlike other parties, the guests do not control the conclusion by when they elect to leave. Instead, the host signals another act in the worship party by collecting the dishes. Once more, this action is a signal that a shift is occurring in the progress of worship. The announcement is an intrusion into the revelry, an intrusion that reminds the Secular Saints that they are not alone, that they live as selves related to all persons and things, present and not present, that it is life in which they revel.

As they return their dishes, the Secular Saints know they are dedicating themselves to offering the possibility, the reception of which they have been celebrating, to everyone who presents himself as the definition of their own selves. The worship party has moved into Act III, the mission of the Secular Saint, and moves rapidly toward the departure of the guests to their own places of residence and existence in society. As they prepare to leave, the Secular Saints may begin to talk of what they plan to do the next day and with whom, but at any rate they affirm their intention to be (and to declare) the liberating Word to all they meet. The benediction (say well) is declared by the host to each as he departs at the door. The worship party has dispersed into all the world.

A casual observer probably would be unable to differentiate the worship party from any other gathering of friends—but the Saints among them know that the meaning of life (Christ) has been present, and that a solemn obligation has been reassumed by everyone who departs at the door. An observer who overheard the talk, however, might well be puzzled by repeated references to God, Christ, and Holy Spirit. He might marvel at the free talk of these religious realities, with no effort to debate the "meaning of God" or the "significance of life." He might, indeed, be perplexed that these ancient words seemed to have assumed meaning for the partygoers, for, like words such as table, atom, and bus, the terms God and Christ are used without definition. What he wouldn't know is that the Secular Saints (a term he wouldn't know either) find the Trinitarian symbols to be every bit as useful as other everyday words of the language. Obviously, these worshipers engage in corporate activities other than the worship party.

The worship party here outlined is clearly not the only form such an affair might take. The worship patterns of any gathering of Secular Saints will be determined by those Saints themselves. But the elements of confession-absolution, celebration, mission will be present, no matter what form they take, for such is the shape of the dramatic enactment of the Holy Spirit life. The number of Saints present is not important; even as few as two or three is sufficient. Whenever Secular Saints encounter each other, worship is the observation. The key is the Christ possibility, not the number or experience of the individuals.

Continuing Evangelism

Vitally important for the Secular Saint is what might be called continuing adult education. The worship party would be impossible if the host and guests did not share an awareness and understanding of the Trinitarian symbols, not to mention a common reception of the Christ possible response to the God activity that defines their selves. Indeed, the worship party would be impossible apart from a common naming of the absolute limits and impossible demands as *God*, the possibility of their goodness as *Christ*, and the reception of that possibility as the *Holy Spirit*. No one does that naming as a matter of course; these symbolic names must be made available.

Christians have long recognized the necessity of study to the life of faith, but often the study has been limited to children. But we are now beginning to realize that the Christ possibility is fully relevant only to mature people, people who are in a position to make free decisions and to be accountable for them. The education of children is an entirely different, though most important, matter from the continuing education of adults.

In discussing the role of the arts in education, Sir Herbert Read observed: "I have in the past written and spoken often enough about the place of the arts in education, and all I have said has been based on the assumption that we are concerned with a growing shoot that will respond as it grows to external influences and disciplinary activities. It seems to me that we are approaching an entirely different problem if growth has come to an end and the object of our attention is no longer tender and labile, but tough and settled in its ways, an adult who has already found his place in the world. Education in such circumstances is no longer the appropriate term: what we must effect may well be a transformation."[9]

Adult education for Secular Sainthood is radically different from the impartation and assimilation of information that is the bulwark of children's education and adult vocational training. It is indeed an effort at transformation. Instead of information or moral instruction, the education of Secular Saints consists of their confrontation with the Christ possibility, a possible response to information that is, at least latently, already present. After all, no one exists who is not aware of himself as confronted with limits and demands. The problem is how to respond to them, or, as the Secular Saint knows, how to respond to God.

Education or study for the Secular Saint could properly be called continuing evangelism, a repeated confrontation with the Christ possibility in the context of reflection on the practical workings of the Holy Spirit. Such continuing evangelism is all but requisite to anything like a worship party, for in worship the Christ possibility is made known in shorthand, by means of symbols—no one at the party needs to have the possibility spelled out, and if he does he does not expect to find it there. Spelling out is the function of education, study, or continuing evangelism.

A curious fact about the Christ possibility, noted earlier, is its essential otherness. A man cannot declare it to himself, although memory can be a significant aid in bringing the ever present possibility to consciousness. The Christ Word comes from the other. Solitary study is tremendously important, as it is in any educational endeavor, but finally the study must be in the company of others engaged in the same pursuit.

Arrangements for corporate study are not always easy for the Secular Saint to make. Schools or colleges for continuing evangelism are few and far between, and those that do exist are often connected with religious orders or communities that attempt to inculcate a particular style of life that the Secular Saint may or may not find difficult to adopt. Schools of theology, designed primarily to train clergymen or academicians, seldom offer courses for continuing evangelism, even though much of the material taught there may be relevant to the Secular Saint. A new type of school is obviously required. Fortunately, schools for the Secular Saint are beginning to emerge in a few spots around the United States and the world, but they vary widely in quality, a fact that indicates the tentative understanding of the Secular Saint and the world he inhabits. A great deal of careful development is yet required.

What would a curriculum of a school for continuing evangelism include? How would it differ from that of a theological seminary or graduate school? The most important difference, upon which every aspect of the school is founded, is its evangelical character, its primary intent to make known the possibility of living as totally free men—within a secular educational framework. Let there be no mistake: the school for continuing evangelism is a *school*, not an indoctrination center. Its purpose is not to cram anything down anyone's throat, but rather, through study of theological and cultural material, to make the Christ possibility repeatedly known. Conducted by Secular Saints, the school is designed to make Secular Sainthood available to men and women. The hope is that students elect the possibility offered, but definitely not that they become evangelists for that life in the way the teachers are, or, in other words, that they become teachers in the school.

The Secular Saint does not necessarily understand his primary vocation to be living so that others may "see and believe." That statement must be carefully understood. In no way does it abrogate the Secular Saint's obligation to be Christ to his neighbor. It simply means the Secular Saint does not go around trying to make *Christians* of others. There is a vast gulf fixed between the two. In the first instance, the Secular Saint is obliged to be consciously (and therefore responsibly) the limit to his neighbor's self. As that limit (God) he is obliged to make known the possibility that the limit comes to the neighbor for his good, he is obliged to be God *incarnate* (Christ) to his neighbor. The obligation stops right there. In the second instance, the man who wants to make Christians of those around him is not content to declare the Christ possibility and then allow the other his own freedom to choose. Instead, the effort is made to ensure a positive decision for Christ—and the evangelist is not satisfied until that positive decision is evident. By so doing, the evangelist attempts to be not only God and Christ to his neighbor, but the Holy Spirit as well. This he cannot be, for the Holy Spirit is present only in the neighbor's free decision, promise, and reduplication. Since that decision cannot be made for him, the effort to do so becomes nothing short of sin on the evangelist's part and places an unnecessary barrier between the neighbor and the Christ possibility. Thus, the Secular Saint knows his primary vocation to be whatever he has chosen it to be in the world. He is first of all a construction worker, lawyer, housewife, clerk, nurse, clergyman, scientist, or whatever. He is, e.g., a clerk who happens to be a Secular Saint, not a Secular Saint who happens to be a clerk.

The sole purpose of the school is (1) to make the Christ life-style a relevant *possibility* to its students; and (2) to conduct continuing conversation on the implications of the Holy Spirit life for the diverse selves of its students.

This dual specific purpose results in a dual curriculum development, with different methods of teaching for each facet. The initial declaration of the Christ possibility is not the same as continuing reflection on the Holy Spirit existence or Secular Sainthood.

Evangelism, or Word-declaring, has become nothing if not problematic by the last half of the twentieth century. The time is long past when a man or woman longed to be saved from eternal damnation. Those are scarce who do not assume that when they die, they are dead. Life after death is not a reality for most people. Hardly anyone worries about whether or not he is going to heaven. Some may *say* this sort of thing is important; they certainly do not act as if it were. It would be nothing short of ridiculous for evangelism to think it had to revive eternal life in order to do its job, an observation so obvious that making it must be justified.

The truth is that contemporary Christians have yet to come to terms with the total demise of the three-story universe. We still find ourselves searching for sophisticated, contemporary ways to preach world-escape as the gospel. What does the gospel mean to a people that is *entirely* of *this* world? If the reader has made his way through to this point in our discourse, he knows how one person, at least, comes at this question. There may be other ways—but whatever they be, they must take the this-worldliness of modern men as a given.

The first part of the curriculum of the school for continuing evangelism is aimed at declaring the gospel in this-worldly terms. This aspect of the curriculum could be called *initial* evangelism, as compared with *continuing* evangelism. It is designed to make the Christ possibility crystal clear, first, to those who think of themselves as Christians, and, second, to those who have consciously rejected Christianity or have not given it serious thought.

An awareness is growing among Secular Saints that the most

fertile mission field is populated by church members. Here are the folk who have lived most obviously by the stop-gap and escape-hatch God. Here are the folk who have yearned for the Holy Spirit to make their decisions for them. But here, also, are the folk who know the biblical stories and who are thus prepared—if reluctant—to hear the gospel those stories bear. In other words, church folk usually have the basic information and inclination to hear the Christ Word through the biblical categories. Large numbers among them, however, have become most unhappy with these categories, have found them inadequate for the wholly secular life they live and find important. Nevertheless, they remain members of the various Roman Catholic and Protestant churches, often for nostalgic, idealistic, social, or guilty reasons. To those church members initial evangelism is addressed. Obviously, they are in no need of membership recruitment; they are already church members.

Initial evangelism is directed also to those who have little or no identity with the Christian faith. It would be a mistake to assume that the Trinitarian symbol structure is totally unfamiliar or neutral for persons who fit into this category—at least in America. Rarely does an individual escape—in contemporary American society— some kind of contact with words such as God, Christ, Holy Ghost, church, etc. They may be words he rebels against, or they may be words simply used by other people, people of a different type than what one would like to be. In each case, the symbols of Christian faith are assumed to point to irrelevant concepts that may help some people but are entirely unnecessary for life as really lived.

Evangelism toward such nonchurchmen is not so very different as might be suspected at first glance. A cliché—"It's harder to talk to church people than to secular men"—has run its course among pastors and other church leaders. Sometimes it has been used to justify failure to address anyone who isn't "safe." Often it has been invoked by those who know little or nothing of secular men. The truth is that nonchurchmen are in just the same need of the Christ possibility as are churchmen, and are neither more nor less receptive to it. But the necessity of *initial* evangelism may, erroneously, appear more obvious.

Participants in the worship party may have received the Christ possibility recently or may be trying to hear it or may be hearing it and rejecting it or may be re-receiving it for the 110th time. But they all have come into direct and conscious contact with it; otherwise they would not show up at a worship party. Conscious encounter with Jesus Christ is the purpose of initial evangelism.

Continuing evangelism is both different from and the same as initial evangelism. It is the same, for the possibility of living as a totally free, responsible individual comes as a new possibility each time it comes. We cannot say often enough that no man ever gets Christ in his pocket as a personal possession to keep forever. Traditional Christian confession, the Secular Saint knows, is mainly the acknowledgment that the Christ possibility has been received (decided upon) but has not been embodied (acted upon). Since it has not been embodied, the fresh presentation of the possibility comes as judgment on past action and a new possibility for active living *every time* it comes. Continuing evangelism, therefore, is for those who have decided for Christ but find they have not embodied him —and what man dares to deny that he has not followed through on his decision?

Nevertheless, continuing evangelism differs from initial evangelism in that human beings are possessed of memory. While the Christ possibility remains a possibility and not a possession, the encounter with it stays in memory. Each time it reappears it brings to consciousness the times it has earlier been present. Thus, continuing evangelism is the re-presentation of Christ, not a brand new presentation of the possibility.

In terms of the curriculum of the school for continuing evangelism, this re-presentation can build on the initial presentation. In other words, the possibility in Jesus Christ can be offered anew in the context of the social sciences, the physical sciences, the arts, philosophy, psychology, or what have you. Never is drama, for example, studied as it would be in a technical drama course or in a course on drama in a literature department. It is always examined in the context of the Christ possibility. What are the options presented by the drama as real possibilities for living? A play such as Edward Albee's *Who's Afraid of Virginia Woolf?* would be examined in a school for continuing evangelism in terms of whether any of the four characters acts out the Christ or the sin response to the situation and whether or not the Christ possibility was made available. If so, at what point? Does the play tell the truth about life as the class members know it? Does it tell a lie? Questions about the author's intentions or what he intended the play to mean are irrelevant to this study. What is important is the word that comes through to the class. Though a literary analysis would ask about the dramatic progression or the adequate characterization or the relationship of *Virginia Woolf* to *Tiny Alice* or *The Zoo Story*, these questions are secondary, if that, in an evangelism school. The school for continuing evangelism exists for the sake of the gospel, nothing else.

In sum, then, when Secular Saints get together they worship and they study. But the two are not always the same activity. Indeed, they may be radically different activities, but they lean on each other, unable to be the vehicle for Secular Sainthood alone. We must not be so simple, however, as to suppose that even the worship party is devoid of study elements. Secular Saints celebrating will talk of what they study, and, in study as such, will talk of how they know worship. Though he may separate his life into various activity spheres, the Secular Saint is a *single* individual.

7

The Corporate Saint

Once I saw mountains angry,
And ranged in battle-front.
Against them stood a little man;
Ay, he was no bigger than my finger.
I laughed, and spoke to one near me,
"Will he prevail?"
"Surely," replied this other;
"His grandfathers beat them many times."
Then did I see much virtue in grandfathers—
At least, for the little man
Who stood against the mountains.

STEPHEN CRANE

HOW IS THE Secular Saint to relate to the parish church? No simple answer is available, because the parish as a social structure no longer exists. The parish church, however, remains as a medieval relic that today is evolving into the Corporate Saint.

The Corporate Saint, a social-action organization of Secular Saints, is very different from the historic parish church and from the congregation of Saints as well, although on occasion the congregation and the Corporate Saint may converge. The congregation of Saints is a casual encounter of Secular Saints with each other, the occasion for celebration, for joy in the Lord, traditionally for worship and fellowship and study. Christ is present in the congregation as the common Lord of the Saints together, and not necessarily in any formal liturgy. The Corporate Saint, on the other hand, is a full-scale organization, incorporated under the laws of the state, that participates in all the organizational details that enable any other organization to perform its assigned tasks.

Furthermore, the concept of the Corporate Saint cuts through all nostalgic attachment to the parish church to a full recognition of the mobility of contemporary man. It suggests centralization of the corporate structure rather than the multiplication of church buildings on the corner of every residential street. It suggests convergence of clergy rather than their isolation in small parish enclaves, and a reduction in the number of professional churchmen with a corresponding increase in the number of professional theologians. The concept of the Corporate Saint suggests the eventual demise of the parish church in the recognition that religion is not a relevant part of contemporary life. The fact remains, however, that the parish church is still very much with us and must be seriously considered by the Secular Saint.

The Secular Saint and the Churches

The Secular Saint lives in a special and peculiar relationship with the social organizations called churches, a relationship he finds both a help and a hindrance to his life as a secularly faithful self. Being both attracted and repelled by the churches, many contemporary Saints vacillate between active support and total rejection of these organizations. The debates by theologians and other churchmen about the nature of the church have not significantly helped the Secular Saint, for his is a very pragmatic problem. Simply put, it is the problem of the usefulness of the churches. And he deserves a serious, worldly reply.

Throughout the ages, the church has been considered the holder of the "keys of the Kingdom of God," the "vicar of Christ," the locus of the Christ possibility. Secular Saints have been told that these descriptions are true even though any particular manifestation of the church is imperfect, partial, and inadequate. But when they see the stones crying out all about them, they wonder. No part of society seems less willing and able to declare the Christ Word than the church—at least to declare it in a way that makes sense to contemporary men. They wonder if it is possible to be a Secular Saint and remain a member of a church. Perhaps Secular Sainthood and church membership are mutually exclusive.

At any particular time for any particular Saint in terms of any particular church it is quite possible that Sainthood and church membership may be incompatible. But whether they are or not depends on the Secular Saint, not on the church. It is time we stopped complaining about the irrelevant church, an activity that assumes the church to be external to those who comprise it. Nevertheless, the validity in this complaining lies precisely in the fact that the church *is* external to its membership. The externality, however, is identical with the externality of any other social organization to its members. It is not a supernatural externality (which makes the church a different order of reality from every other organization) that prohibits organized reformulation.

That social structures become more than simply the collective will of those who constitute them or even of those who administer them is readily apparent to any observer of complex twentieth-century culture. A giant corporation, for instance, takes on an image that remains more or less constant through year after year of stockholders' voting and countless changes in administrative personnel.

Alteration in management practices and product appearance and type do take place, but without anyone being able to isolate credit or blame for the change. The corporation has, so it seems, a life of its own. In other words, the corporation does not depend for its existence upon any one person or group of persons (although obviously it cannot exist with no persons at all).

Perhaps more than private corporations, governments assume an autonomous character. The adage, "You can't fight city hall," points in the direction of government's externality. Efforts to affect the foreign policy of the United States appear to be futile gestures. A friend of mine put it well when he observed that the administration was like a sheet hung on a line. One throws a ball against it, the sheet gives, but when the ball drops to the ground, the sheet returns to its former position and shape. Instead of throwing at the sheet, one should attack the line or the poles that support it. Governments are not immortal, as the actuality of successful revolution reveals. But even then, a new and often similar government arises to take the place of the old. Revolutions are fought, usually, against the system, an impersonal but highly powerful reality. While a single individual or group may be singled out as the specific target, they are not attacked as persons (although the revolutionaries probably believe they are). Instead, they are attacked as symbols of the system, which is independent of and external to those who comprise the society and, finally, to those directly responsible for administration of it.

While governments are contexts in which everyone lives simply by the sociological facts of birth, the churches of contemporary America are entirely voluntary. Rebellion against them is unnecessary—because they do not exercise the power of life and death, health and sickness, wealth and poverty. If I find I cannot live within Church A, I can always become part of Church B or of no church at all. No longer does the church have the say about my eternal destiny.

The Secular Saint, therefore, is free to live and work within a church organization or not. Neither the society at large nor his friends and colleagues will pass judgment should he make either choice. Church membership is as optional for him as civic club or professional society membership. His criterion is always whether or not such membership is the most advantageous avenue for accomplishing what he wishes to accomplish.

It would be nice if we could simply leave the question of the Secular Saint's relation to the churches here, but the problem is actually far more complicated. The churches are organizations among organizations, true, but they are the organizations, nevertheless, that preach the Word and administer the sacraments. They are in the business of making the Christ possibility available and are the link with the communion of Saints throughout time. Also, they are frequently the places from which the Secular Saint has heard the Word that freed him from dependency upon any organization or community for his life's significance. The Secular Saint may thus remain convinced that the churches hold a claim prior to that of other organizations for his allegiance and support. He may find himself in a position analogous to the adult who knows he is free of parental control but still feels obliged to act as his parents would want him to act. He knows that his genuine responsibility to history and his fellows lies more in his relationship to his children than to his parents, but the parents still lay their prior claim upon him, both directly and implied.

The recognition that the churches are organizations among organizations is a continual necessity for the Secular Saint, because he keeps slipping in and out of his promise to find life to be good without handing that most important decision over to some man, circumstance, or principle—or to a church, where the Christ Word is declared in the powerful historic symbols. The Secular Saint may find himself acting as though he owes absolute allegiance to the person or group from which he heard—and then accepted—the Christ possibility. Nevertheless, he knows that his response and his servanthood are focused on Christ, not on the particular point at which the possibility is encountered. The Secular Saint is free from the churches, a freedom that allows him to declare the Christ possibility to them, as he is free to declare it to every other part of his self.

In the previous chapter, I outlined the various understandings that have informed the church in the past. I suggested that "people of God" was no longer adequate for contemporary Secular Saints, but that "communion of Saints," when coupled with "congregation of Saints," was a most helpful image. The difficulty the Secular Saint experiences with the parish church is its apparent inability to relinquish the people of God image, even though by so doing it knows itself to be caught in a downdraft that will eventually force it from the historical scene. The phenomenon of congregations moving from the city to the suburbs, because the membership has moved or because the suburbs seem to have more religious people, is now commonplace. I am reminded of the similar activity of major-league baseball teams, which now seem to think the way to keep their financial affairs in order is to move from city to city as attendance falls off at their present location. In neither instance is the maneuver destined to accomplish its intended purpose: the grass seldom turns out to be greener in the other yard.

A fact of our time is that men and women do not live in communities, and no attempt to make them live in communities will be successful. The opposite result is most likely to occur: the most alert and creative persons will simply find their more significant social involvement elsewhere. Here lies an important fact about the new individual, the Secular Saint. While he does not live in communities, with their close-knit ties of history, blood, race, and cult, he does live in collectives, with their orientation toward goals, purposes, significant ends.

I am aware that collective is a dangerous word, for in American society it is associated with Marxist ideology, or communism, which is perhaps the most pejorative term presently available. But collective is, quite apart from Karl Marx, the most descriptive term available for the type of group activities that now grace the American historical scene. Just what is a collective?

A collective, unlike a community, is a collection of people who choose to band together in order to accomplish a particular task. The task need not be of great moment, but may, in fact, be quite simple, such as joint ownership of a sailboat. Such joint ownership may be the only direct association the members of the collective have with one another, but it is for that reason no less important. After all, no one expects to develop lasting friendships in the collective. When the boat sinks or when one or more of the partners move to a distant city, the collective collapses—and no one is surprised or bothered about it.

The congregation of Saints is such a collective. Like the boat owners, Secular Saints have only one thing in common: reception of the Christ possible response to life. That is absolutely everything necessary for their association. An important difference between the congregation of Saints and the sailboat collective, however, is that in the former the boat does not sink. Partners may move away, but the boat remains afloat; the Christ possibility is always already present to each of them, no matter where he happens to be or under what circumstances. Secular Saints, however, do not remain within a particular congregation of Saints if they discern that the congregation is failing to be responsible to Jesus Christ, just as a boat partner may well sell his interest quickly if he discovers that his partners refuse to keep the boat in proper condition.

We must not be alarmed, therefore, when Secular Saints find they cannot be part of parish churches that persist in acting as though the reason for their being is to create and maintain close personal relationship among the members. Caught, as our society presently is, in a major attempt to develop equal rights for all citizens, no matter their color or racial background, sizable numbers of Secular Saints have elected to join parish churches in so-called changing neighborhoods in order to witness to the validity of genuinely interracial living. These persons have not been limited, of course, either to whites or Negroes. White Secular Saints have chosen to live and participate in churches in predominantly Negro neighborhoods, and Negro Secular Saints have made strenuous efforts to participate in churches of predominantly white neighborhoods. But a curious development has occurred. Some of each group are now finding out that they simply don't "fit in," and the reasons seldom have anything particular to do with race. For when a man discovers that members of other races are human beings who have the same problems and faults as those of his own hue, he discovers that he cannot "like" all Negroes or all whites. Moving as he does among a variety of collectives every day, he begins to develop friendships beyond the borders of his residential neighborhood and the confines of his local church. He often wishes he could join a church where he could associate with some of the people he has come to know and like in other connections—but his sense of guilt at leaving the interracial congregation keeps him where he is, and miserable.

When he "comes to himself," the Secular Saint in this type of situation knows he is free to choose his congregation as he wills and for whatever reasons he wishes. The guilt is gone. This is a decision he does not take lightly, however. He does, indeed, "observe, judge, weigh-up, and decide" before he acts. And in so doing, he fulfills his responsibility both to the congregation he leaves and the one to which he comes.

Probably the most distressing characteristic of the parish church is its standard for judging itself a success or a failure. The usual standard is the degree of warm, interpersonal relationships that have developed among members, and the number and diversity of congregational activities. Members are supposed to understand themselves as responsible to each other for the sake of the parish church's vitality. When this vitality fades, the members rightly consider each other to have let the church down, and usually try to work a little harder in order to get things going again. But the attempt is seldom successful, because the judgment standard is incompatible with the society in which the parish exists.

Few serious commentators on the parish structure today fail to note that the pattern has outlived its usefulness. When it developed during the Middle Ages, the parish plan for church organization made real sense, for the church was the center of social existence. People came from all around to mass and other social events held at the cathedral, which had been abuilding for yea these many years. The mobility of modern man was undreamed of; most men never traveled more than the distance from their homes to the village. The parish, therefore, was a clearly identifiable geographic and sociological unit. The contemporary parish is no such thing. Members of a congregation often live many miles from the parish meeting-house and have no direct association with those they see there other than through parish activities. Mothers who object strongly to the breakdown in the neighborhood school system have no hesitancy in driving five or ten miles to Sunday school. This kind of situation is not conducive to the close personal relationships of the community; it is appropriate to the collective.

We could ask why people continue to attend a church far from their residence. The reasons vary from pure sentimentality to the type of social concern present in members of interracial churches many blocks away from their homes. But whatever the reasons, the parish already approaches the collective or secular organization pattern rather than the community or religious fellowship pattern.

The collective may be simple and rather informal, like the sailboat partners, or it may be a highly complicated institutionalized organization, such as an agricultural cooperative, but whatever its size or shape, it exists because of one or more common interests or goals on the part of those who constitute it. Moreover, this interest or goal is *brought to* the collective by the constituents, a condition which is infinitely different from the parish structure, in which the members are uniformly hoping *to gain* something from their membership that they do not presently possess.

Personal conflict in a collective, therefore, takes on a different cast than it does in the parish or community. For personal conflict—which does indeed exist, and is frequently very bitter—can be contained within the structure of the organization and related directly to the organization's goals and purposes. If the conflict becomes so acute as to jeopardize the purposes of the collective, a decision can be made about who will go and who will stay. Once that decision has been made, the organization can revert to doing the job it is designed to do.

But in the parish, interpersonal harmony is itself the goal. "Men and women today look to the local congregation as a haven from conflict and tension," Gibson Winter writes. "Clergymen view their work as the maintenance of harmonious relationships within the flock; the frictionless machine is the ideal image of the congregation. The creation of such *harmonious enclaves* is an indication of the utter dislocation of the Church in our society."[1] Since this is the case, personal conflict is disruptive of the parish; eviction of members would be a confession of failure, as is the typical resolution of such conflicts: the voluntary resignation of one or more parties to the dispute, by which the parish is further impoverished.

We should not be surprised that the Roman Catholic Church, in which excommunication is always possible, has had a significantly greater measure of success in the organizational world than have the free or confessional churches.

The distinction between the community and the collective is blurred by the fact that collectives frequently develop many of the manifestations of community. Friendships, for instance, are common among people who work together on a common project. Occasionally these friendships continue beyond the association of the collective, but their intensity is almost always diminished. On the other hand, friendships within a collective sometimes have the facility for deeper development than is the case in communities. Everyone is familiar with the feeling that he or she must be careful not to have too many contacts with so-and-so because they are getting to know each other so well that signs of potential conflict are visible. In order to protect the friendship, the ties must consciously be loosened without the other person being apprised of what is going on. Constituents of a collective, however, are free to enter as deeply as they wish into the lives of their colleagues, because their basic relationship is founded on the more or less objective goal of the organization and not upon the friendship itself.

The Secular Saint flourishes in the collective, for the collective sets him free to be the single individual he knows himself to be in Christ. And, conversely, his Secular Sainthood frees him to participate fully in the collective endeavors of his society. If only the church were a collective rather than a community!

Already the churches, in their denominational superstructures, are collective in practical operation. Like other organizations or institutionalized collectives, the churches are run by professionals who are ranked on status levels. I will use The Methodist Church as an illustration, not only because it is most familiar to me, but because it is one of the most extensive ecclesiastical organizations ever to emerge outside Roman Catholicism. Methodism poses two status structures. One, related to the administration of the parish church, includes ministers, district superintendents, and bishops. The other, supportive of the parish church (but ranging wider in actual practice), includes board and agency secretaries and staffs, plus co-opted specialists. Whereas the first status structure is composed exclusively of clergy, the second includes both clergy and nonclergy, with no particular status distinction hinging on ordination.

Both structures are composed of professionals who derive their financial support from the church membership, which is not composed of ecclesiastical professionals. Unlike stockholders in a corporation, the church membership does not expect to derive a financial return from its support of these organizational structures. Instead, it expects to derive spiritual benefits. The fact that the dividends are to be paid in different currency in no way affects the correspondence of organizational patterns. Nevertheless, a strange myth persists, enhanced by the "lay movement" that has attracted a good deal of attention since 1945, that The Methodist Church and other Protestant religious organizations are *really* run by laymen (nonprofessionals), or, if they are not, they should be. The fact is that most churches are not run by laymen and cannot possibly be conducted by them. In order to function as an organization among organizations in twentieth-century America, they must be administered by professionals. No comparable cultural organization operates without professional management—not government, not education, not industry, not medicine.

The board and agency structure is openly professional, with status and promotion based more or less on ability and performance. Specialists and generalists within this structure work in office buildings, keep office hours, and in general operate as do professionals in any other field. Bishops and district superintendents, in the parish supervision structure, also tend to operate professionally and understand themselves to be professionals. They take for granted that they need and deserve the requisite tools for their job, from office equipment to travel funds to competent secretarial and staff assistance. Only the parish minister is left in a frankly ambiguous position. Trained in professional schools (seminaries) to be theological experts, parish ministers find themselves under pressure to be business managers, psychologists, janitors, almost anything but theologians. A persistent problem of seminaries and their students is the observable fact that many graduates retain very little of their theological training. Actually, no one should be surprised at this fact, for, even though they may decry it, seminary students know they will not be held accountable for their theology when they later conduct their ministry. The parish minister therefore is often frustrated in his professional life, coming to believe that he is not really qualified to be a theologian after all, and must become another kind of professional, for which experience is the only school: the professional churchman. The parish minister is caught in the no-man's-land between the organizational collective and the communal parish, and, let no one be deceived, his decision about where he will come down is very difficult. Bishops and board secretaries are professional churchmen (not professional theologians), too, but they are higher on the status scale and therefore farther removed from the particular professional image conflict faced by the parish minister. The latter must move back and forth between the two images —until the day comes when he decides to *be* either one or the other.

The present Protestant denominations are a mixture of collective and community, with the collective rationalized on the basis that it serves or supports the community, which is actually what the church is supposed to be all about. The trouble is that at no level is the role of the professional theologian effectively combined with the role of the professional churchman or administrator; and the level where the combination is assumed to take place is lowest on the status pole, where organizational protection is weakest.

The professional levels in The Methodist Church (which are paralleled in most Protestant denominations) reveal some of the problems that emerge when the implications of collective-communal conflict take practical shape. The parish is member-oriented; the collective is staff-oriented. The parish is emotion-oriented; the collective is objective-oriented. The parish is *served* by ministers; the collective is *staffed* by executives.

Occasionally, someone comes up with the notion that clergy who work on board and agency staffs should periodically return to the parish in order "to find out what's really going on." The idea fails to catch on because staff people know, often without consciously being aware of it, that what's really going on is much more likely to be found in the board or agency than in the parish. They know that the decisions that really affect the lives of people in this nation are made in organizational collectives, and not in communal parishes. But both agency staffs and parish ministers persist in maintaining the fiction that the opposite is true. Until they stop doing so, little change is likely to take place in denominational activity and organization—and the Christ possibility will continue to be encapsulated in a community context that hinders, at least, its reception by contemporary men and women.

Movements toward "church renewal" have been rife in recent years, but, with few exceptions, they have come to nought because they made the false assumption that change could come only from the bottom up. Get the people converted to Secular Sainthood, so to speak, and they will insist that the church structure be changed. It simply doesn't happen this way. What does happen is that Secular Saints emerge from the creative parishes and lay training institutes to go out and live as Secular Saints, frustrated at the lack of significance in the parish church but wanting to put their main efforts in places where they will make more impact.

And yet, in all the talk about "church renewal" and the "ministry of the laity" and "new forms of the church," the emergence of these Secular Saints, who live the Holy Spirit life without the support of organizations, no matter how molecular, has scarcely been noticed. In a world where the atom is being split into ever smaller pieces, is it any wonder that Christ should come to rest in the Secular Saint rather than the people of God? Today the Christ embodiment is not placed in the church as the local congregation; it is placed in the Secular Saint, and that very fact has called into question all the organizations called "church." The contemporary world may now begin to see the replacement of "church" with "Corporate Saint," in the same way that St. Paul's day saw, without knowing it, the replacement of "people of God" with "communion of Saints." Secular Saints are in a unique position (if they choose to involve themselves with a church organization) to break through the present inertia by insisting that everything the parish church does be aimed toward making the Christ possibility relevantly available. By so doing, they will be taking the next logical step from Secular Sainthood: support of the Corporate Saint, which is the evolution of the churches into a new and more adequate form for the steady-state world.

The Corporate Saint

Those who would speak of corporate Christian life in terms other than the parish often fall into the trap of envisioning the new structure on the basis of the way it "ought to be," and then suggesting that the new form can become reality if only the intransigents in the present church forms come around, or if some kind of revolution takes place from below to cast off the old garment and joyfully put on the new. Unfortunately, change refuses to take place in this way, at least in American society. Even the Negro revolution, the most obvious revolutionary movement in recent days, is failing to effect the desired change with anything like the rapidity it deserves. Certainly, change does not take place within the Protestant establishment in a revolutionary way.

On the other hand, we have learned that if we wait for significant change to occur in the denominations by the normal route—innovative persons working their way into the power structure and there bringing alteration by infiltration—we wait till palm trees grow in Little America. But there is another way: planned evolution.

Evolution evokes a picture of gradual, imperceptible change. But it need not necessarily be so. Perhaps the leap from one plateau to the next that Bergson imagined for nature is more appropriate. Evolution can be quite dramatic, but in a different way from the drama of revolution. Evolution, unlike revolution, does not break with the past ways so that they are disvalued (or preserved only as historical monuments) so much as it allows the past or present forms to change themselves into what later is seen to be an entirely new form. Planned evolution is simply evolution in the normal sense with a bit of human vision added. John R. Platt, a biophysicist who has written a remarkable book entitled *The Step to Man*, speaks of evolution in a manner that reveals him as a Secular Saint:

> For this unique past, yours and mine, surely makes possible some unique things we can do in the present, starting here. Life flings us out randomly like seeds into all sorts of crevices, high and low. Some fall on rocks and some among thorns, while others have the still worse fate of being overnourished and overprotected. But the evolutionary hope is that every seed, by its very combination of accidents, will find in itself some new potentiality

for development that will enlarge the experience of the whole race. We have regarded the survival of the fittest as a cruel doctrine; but it is a doctrine of life as much as a doctrine of death. It means the survival of wing and brain, of the most adaptable, the most enduring, the most anticipatory, the most enjoying, the most diversely communicating with the universe. The picture of man's evolution is not that of a huddled community waiting to be eaten, but that of explorers always learning how to live beyond the fringes. In the rock itself, one tough flower may find a hard niche that in a time of storms preserves the species. What seemed catastrophe becomes the single hope of salvation.[2]

There exists with the parish a new potentiality for development that will produce—and is already producing—the Corporate Saint. It is the Christian faith itself. The trust that life is very good and may be lived as such has been nurtured in the seminaries and the parishes all along; the flame has never completely died, and recently has begun to burn brighter. For the first time in many a theological generation, clergy who have been in parish churches for ten to twenty years have not lost the reforming zeal they brought with them to their first church. Many of their colleagues have dropped along the way, but enough remain who search for a new day that there is hope for its arrival.

No purpose ever existed, really, for the parish church other than the declaration of the gospel, and this, too, is the purpose of the collective Corporate Saint. Secular Saints have some great good news to tell—and nothing short of the most effective organizational structure is sufficient for getting that news around. Thus, while Secular Saints will always work and live within a multitude of collectives that have a variety of purposes, the sole purpose of the Corporate Saint is to make the Christ possible response to the limits and demands of human existence available for the choosing of as many people as possible. Thus, the most potent potentiality for development still lies in the Word that constitutes the significance of all things.

In addition, however, the parish structure possesses a great deal of latent social power itself.

What corporation would not give its eyeteeth for a merchandising network such as the Christian faith possesses in the parish system! Like the dinosaur, which lived happily as long as water covered the earth to support its immense weight, but died when the waters receded, the parish system flourished so long as the society into which it was born remained more or less intact, but now hardly knows what to do with its white elephant buildings and isolated clergy with their struggling congregations. Nevertheless, it is those very buildings and clergy and congregations that have the potential to become the Corporate Saint.

But perhaps the greatest organizational potential for the Corporate Saint is present in the evolutionary step that has already created the board and agency structure of the denominations. Here is the organization model for the Corporate Saint, the "parish" of tomorrow. Wherever it comes into being, the Corporate Saint will be realized through the cooperation of parish ministers, parish members, and denominational supraparish organizations. It will evolve both from the bottom up and from the top down, incorporating the relevant functions of the present parish church into a thoroughgoing organizational collective. The specific requirements upon any particular Corporate Saint are never identical with those of others. Nevertheless, the organizational pattern, developed on the model of business and industry, presently utilized by the boards and agencies of the denominations, is flexible enough to handle any such specific needs.

One of the pragmatic difficulties with the parish church (apart from the fact that no one actually lives in parishes anymore, certainly not those who dwell in metropolitan areas) is its extremely localized character. Most Protestant denominations have long since given up trying to delineate parish boundaries, beyond which a parish is not supposed to draw members. In a day in which people shop for churches in the same way they shop for automobiles, such efforts would be futile in any case. The result has been the close proximity of churches of different denominations and even of the same denomination. It is not too uncommon to have two church buildings of the same denomination within a few blocks of each other, if not on the same block. Parish churches tend, therefore, to limit their activities, not to the people who live in the geographic area, but to the membership of the churches, and the minister is supposed to serve the members, scattered as they are. Churches recognize this fact by providing automobile expense allowance for their ministers.

Most Protestant churches struggle to keep their buildings in repair and to pay their minister a salary that is more or less adequate for himself and his family. And since maintaining the parish church organization often requires a great deal of effort and in some cases financial sacrifice on the part of the church "pillars," members of the congregation quite naturally come to expect the minister who is the recipient of this sacrifice to perform the duties they have paid him to perform. The minister, as we have seen, is caught in a terrible bind if his understanding of his responsibilities differs from that of his congregation. Often, resentment begins to build within the parish minister as he realizes that he can never reach the status his long years in school and his professional competence would seem to assure him. Public opinion polls continue to list the clergyman farther and farther down the status list; the day that knew no genuine professional other than the clergyman is lost in the historical mists. The minister is left with a nominally important position within the community (he is asked to pronounce the invocation at high school football games), but is actually expected to follow the wishes of influential laymen.

Wisdom may have resided in the clergymen who pressured Congress to classify them as self-employed persons relative to Social Security, even though that classification is more expensive to them when it comes time to pay their annual tax. The gesture signified that the minister is, in fact, his own man. He may serve a congregation, but he serves it in his own way. The English have for generations denominated the money paid to a clergyman—and by extension the parish church itself—a "living," by which they have symbolized the fact that clergy are *given* enough upon which to live in order that they may be free of economic concerns to proclaim the gospel. This understanding is no longer reality; today ministers are employees of parish churches in the same way janitors are, and are expected to follow the directions of the governing body of the parish. Here again is an illustration of the churches moving away from the parish image pure and simple toward the organizational image of the contemporary world.

The conflict between these two images of the theological professional is resolved in the Corporate Saint. No longer is the minister a minister; he is a professional theologian, with special abilities within the organizational structure. Instead of remaining isolated in a parish church, he becomes part of a staff of professionals who are committed to proclaiming the gospel to a large segment of the population, but specialized according to interest and training. How can this be? Let us take a look at the essential elements of the Corporate Saint.

Worship is an element in the life of the Secular Saint, whether it be in the medieval cathedral or the worship party in his home. I have suggested earlier that the Secular Saint has no particular need to worship in the regular way assumed by the schedule of parish churches, worshiping instead in the highly self-conscious but informal congregation of Saints. But the *communion* of Saints requires that he occasionally worship in the formal and liturgical fashion of his fathers, updated perhaps, but still incorporating the liturgical forms that clue him in that he stands alongside those who have gone before and those who will come. Worship, therefore, is a part of the responsibility of the Corporate Saint, a part of its declaration of the gospel.

Likewise, the school for continuing evangelism cannot be left to the caprice of the congregation of Saints, because the congregation is not able to handle the intricacies of conducting a school. The traditional study function of the church must reside with the Corporate Saint, as well as initial presentation of the Christ possibility in formal fashion.

The third element that must be part of any contemporary corporate structure of Secular Saints is social action. The time is long past when we could believe that the social context in which we live is not relevant to the Christian faith, for we know with certainty today that the Christ possibility is seldom heard in a social context that does not provide for basic necessities of human existence. The Corporate Saint is structured to work at developing a social context in which the Christ Word may be heard to best advantage.

No matter what its specific form, the Corporate Saint includes organizational mechanisms for ensuring that worship, evangelism (including education), and social action for the sake of the Christ possibility take place. It is with this necessity in mind that the following organizational pattern for the Corporate Saint is suggested. Since we live in collectives today instead of communities, the Corporate Saint is designed to touch persons living in as large a geographical area as possible with its programming. Consequently, a Corporate Saint addresses itself to persons living and working in at least one-fourth of a metropolitan area or an entire trade area in nonmetropolitan sections of the country. Obviously, an area this size will encompass the jurisdictions of many parish churches, each of which becomes a part of the Corporate Saint and delegates to it the major part of its activity.

The evolution of the parish church into the Corporate Saint, then, does not begin with the elimination of the church. It begins with the church governing body agreeing to cooperate with other churches in the creation of a new organization, the Corporate Saint, that can most effectively reach the largest number of people in the area the parishes present consider their own. Two parish churches would be sufficient to begin a Corporate Saint, although the larger the number the more hopeful the prognosis for the new organization's success. By agreeing to cooperate in the new, area-wide organization, the parish church gives its minister permission to become a staff member of the Corporate Saint and to devote the majority of his time to developing and implementing the programming of the new organization.

A board of directors for the Corporate Saint could be composed of members elected by the appropriate bodies in the parish churches, which board would then become the legal and functional policy-setting body for the multiparish organization. Ministers of the churches—now the staff of the Corporate Saint—would be expected to operate in the context of policy established by the board. The board would, as time went on, choose its own staff members as new staff is added or as replacements become necessary. Such choices would be made on the basis of competence for the position being filled, not on the basis of ordination or seniority with ecclesiastical establishments. Difficulties naturally will arise with the various

THE CORPORATE SAINT — A Suggested Organizational Pattern

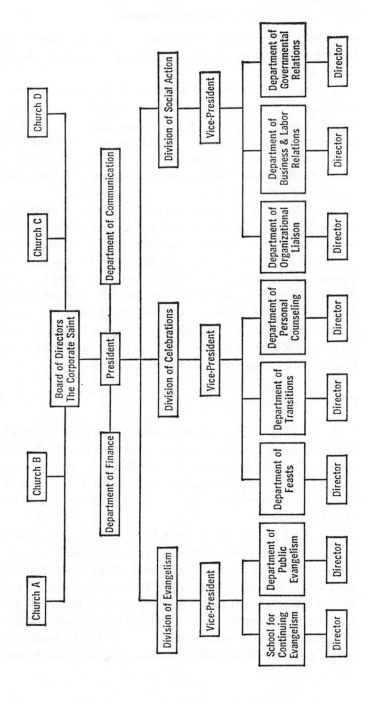

denominational methods of assigning clergy, but these can be handled with a minimum of conflict if the evolutionary principle is clearly understood.

In order to get as detailed a picture of the Corporate Saint as possible, let us assume that at least four parish churches elect to cooperate in the formation of a Corporate Saint, and, further, let us assume that they are rather widely separated within an area roughly one-fourth the size of a metropolitan area such as Kansas City or Washington, D.C. For practical purposes, all four churches are affiliated with the same Protestant denomination.

The organization chart on the preceding page pictures the formal structure of a possible Corporate Saint. Unless sufficient funds are available to secure a fifth staff member, one of the four clergy is elected president of the Corporate Saint, with the responsibility of representing the staff before the board and supervising the work of the staff in the conduct of their own responsibilities. The president is the major morale figure on the staff, the person who sees to it that the overall vision of the Corporate Saint is kept in focus. It is his responsibility, also, to provide for the public image of the organization and to manage the total financial situation.

Evangelism

The Division of Evangelism, headed by a vice-president of the Corporate Saint and staffed by as many department directors as necessary (and for which funds are available), is responsible for the school for continuing evangelism and for public meetings of all kinds other than those specifically lodged in the Division of Celebrations.

The school for continuing evangelism should have two divisions, one for adults (including teen-agers) and one for children. Depending on the clientele of the Corporate Saint, the curriculum of the adult school will range from highly intellectual to almost entirely nonverbal content, but, however it is presented, the school will be dedicated to making the Christ possibility known, both initially and continually. In each case, particularly the latter, Secular Saints gather to reflect on the life of Secular Sainthood and to become aware of diverse avenues for becoming aware of the relationship matrices that comprise their selves.

Initial evangelism will focus on the meaning of the Christ possibility almost exclusively, in terms of which "God" and "Holy Spirit" become relevant. Radically different from traditional Bible study, initial evangelism is based on the assumption that no one reads the Bible—or comprehends the significance in the events that define his existence—unless he does so through some set of presuppositions, some symbol system that allows him to see and understand some things and blocks out others. Thus, initial evangelism is an attempt to look at the conceptual framework within which contemporary men and women relate to their world, and to offer the Christ possibility as a genuine alternative. Once more, the school for continuing evangelism is quite definitely a school, not an indoctrination center. The Christ possibility is made known and the effort is made to present it as a viable option, but no attempt is made to force it down anyone's throat. Faculty of the school must always be willing to allow students to walk away, as the rich young man did from Jesus.

Continuing evangelism in the adult school assumes that students have been confronted with the Christ possibility at least once, by virtue of the fact that they have elected to attend classes in initial evangelism. Further, courses in continuing evangelism are composed of Secular Saints who wish to delve deeper into the implications of Secular Sainthood. The content of these courses, therefore, is far different from those in initial evangelism. Instead of concentrating on the Christ possibility, teachers examine with the Secular Saints the implications of the Holy Spirit life in the various collective contexts in which all of them live. The physical sciences, the social sciences, psychology, art, literature, music, almost any cultural discipline is available for concentrated study by the Secular Saints. In the course of continuing evangelism, the Christ possibility is revealed as being present at all points in all areas of human existence.

The school for continuing evangelism also may take advantage of its continuing courses to examine the power concentrations and points of potential influence in the city, state, and nation, and to develop ways by which the Secular Saints, both individually and together, may act to alter social conditions so that the great good news in Jesus Christ may be heard. The school is one of the points at which the Corporate Saint directly impinges upon the congregation of Saints and the congregation encounters the Corporate Saint directly. For the Saints have indeed gathered when they attend courses in continuing evangelism, and the gathering is a most important part of their Secular Sainthood, though by no means is it mandatory. We must never forget that Secular Saints may quite logically choose to have nothing to do with the Corporate Saint or with any formal congregation of Saints (though informal congregation is a natural part of their existence, without which they would, by definition, not be Secular Saints at all).

The children's school of the Corporate Saint moves in a different direction than does the adult school, for children are simply not in a position to understand or respond to the Christ possibility. Secular Sainthood is for adults. But children need to become familiar with the biblical literature and the history of the Christian church and to be introduced to the historic dogmas and creeds. The time may well come in the United States when this education will take place in the public schools, as the society as a whole recognizes that no person can understand Western civilization without a working knowledge of the way in which the church, including its doctrine, has influenced contemporary culture. But this time is yet to be reached, and until it is the Corporate Saint must continue to fill the gap—for the sake of the reception of the Christ possibility when that possibility becomes relevant. I should note at this point that teen-agers and youth are not children. The age at which the limits and demands of life become conscious and demand a responsible decision is lower than it has ever been. High school students are, in most cases, every bit as mature in their thinking and potential action as most older adults. They should be invited to attend the adult school in classes composed of their peers and also in classes of older adults.

What happens to the Sunday school in the collective school for continuing evangelism? No intrinsic reason exists for not holding the children's school on Sunday morning. But the tradition of Sunday school being little more than baby-sitting is very hard to overcome. Consequently, the school often could be more advantageous when held after public school hours one or more days per week. But the insistence should be rigorous that the children's school is a *school*, at which attendance is regular. Payment of a tuition fee makes this requirement more visible, particularly if the school is held on Sunday morning. Scholarship funds may be made available for those who have difficulty paying the tuition fee, but they should not be dispensed save upon formal application.

One of the difficulties every Sunday school faces is the scarcity of trained teachers. The school for continuing evangelism should not expect to be exempt from that trouble either, particularly in its early years. For this reason, the staff of the Corporate Saint should be prepared to teach in the children's school just as it does in the adult school, which may mean some additional schooling on their part, too. As the adult school proceeds, teachers for the children's school will doubtless emerge from among the Secular Saints, in which case, the staff must conduct classes in pedagogy and curriculum in order thoroughly to train Secular Saints for this specialized task. Persons who assume teaching duties should be hired on a pay scale comparable with that of public school teachers, although dedication to Secular Sainthood is a *sine qua non* for faculty membership. The Corporate Saint is not a volunteer organization.

The Department of Public Evangelism is responsible for making the Christ possibility known far and wide through means less disciplined than the school for continuing evangelism. This department could sponsor lectureships, concerts, plays, poetry readings, cinema showings, art exhibits, and the like, as well as two- or three-day seminars in ethics, art, government, science, etc. The department, in other words, is responsible for keeping the service area alert to the possibilities for highly significant life that already exist in the culture. While opportunities for discussion should always be available at lectures and art exhibits, for example, these should not be the main purpose. The speech or the art must carry its own weight. The Department of Public Evangelism is not in the business of speaking in "God language"; it is in the business of offering the "stones" that cry out from every corner of our universe that life is good and may be received as such. No week should go by without the department sponsoring one or more area-wide events, which should be widely publicized. The possibilities are all but endless.

Another possibility for this department is the employment of roving evangelists, who will spend their time at places where people naturally gather—bars, restaurants, hotels, PTA's, civic clubs, etc.— simply listening to talk and making the Christ possibility available, in words when possible, and by their presence when it is not. These people should be readily identifiable as Secular Saints in the employ of the Corporate Saint, but they should not be recruiters for the school for continuing evangelism or for any of the other programming of the Corporate Saint (although this may well be a result of their presence). Their main objective is to make certain that as many people as possible encounter the Christ possible response to their lives and make a choice relative to it.

Celebrations

The presence of the Division of Celebrations within the Corporate Saint represents the social necessity for public symbolization of Secular Sainthood and the periodic declaration that Christian faith is something of which its adherents are proud indeed. This element is particularly present in the Department of Feasts, whose responsibility is to conduct massive worship services on the high festival days of the Christian year. By so doing, the department keeps before the public, as well as the Secular Saints, the fact that the Christ possibility is present constantly in the midst of the society as a genuine option for all men's choosing. Depending on the season of the Christian year, these celebrations will be sober or gay, but they will always be occasions for joyful declaration that Christ is the actual Lord of the universe.

High festival celebrations are categorically different from the worship party or the informal gathering of Secular Saints in daily visits. Festivals utilize the symbols of the faith quite openly and without apology to all those who choose to come. They need not maintain medieval imagery (although they may on occasion), but may incorporate contemporary music, dance, drama, and verbal symbols; they are celebrations, in which all the stops are pulled out, that require careful planning and execution.

If the service area is large enough, several locations may be selected for the celebration of any particular feast, but the number should not be too great, lest the celebration turn into what looks like simply another Sunday worship service of the parish church. These feasts should be widely publicized for some time in advance, and the attendance should be as large as possible. In time, the residents of the area will come to anticipate the celebration and will plan their own schedules to allow them to celebrate with others at these times.

The Department of Transitions is properly part of the Division of Celebrations, for baptisms, weddings, and funerals are unique celebrations in the lives of individuals, as contrasted with public celebrations on high festival days. The staff of the Corporate Saint should work through for itself the meaning of these personal celebrations and should be adequately prepared to help the individuals concerned toward a thorough understanding of them, too.

The mid-twentieth century has little need for elaborate initiation rites, and the Secular Saint certainly finds no use for them. What conceivable purpose could baptism have, therefore, in the life either of the Secular Saint or the Corporate Saint? This is not the place for a full-scale discussion of baptism, but it is the place to note that baptism is the visible sign of a person's choice to enter the communion of Saints (not the congregation of Saints). Since neither the congregation of Saints—which may not be organized at all—nor the Corporate Saint holds the keys to the Kingdom of God, and thus cannot permit or prohibit entry into the communion of Saints, baptism through either one becomes problematic. Its role, however, remains quite significant for the Secular Saint who chooses it, in which case it symbolizes his decision to live the Holy Spirit life. The rite becomes the stone that always stands in judgment upon him. In the case of infant baptism, the rite symbolizes the parent's or guardian's decision to train his child as best he can in the background of the Christian faith and constantly to hold the Christ possibility before him. The Corporate Saint, through its Department of Transitions, stands ready to make baptism one of the most significant events in the life of the Secular Saint—if he chooses to participate in it. Every effort should be made to avoid the perfunctory baptisms that customarily are now held in the parish church. Baptism is not something to be gotten through; it is a high personal festival in which the gathered Saints share.

Likewise, weddings are symbols of a change in life-styles on the part of those being married. The Department of Transitions should be prepared to help persons about to be married arrive at a responsible understanding of sex and family relationships, as well as a clear understanding of the symbolic significance of marriage itself. This significance is not at all certain in contemporary society, and the staff of the Corporate Saint must be careful not to make any easy assumptions at this point. Marriage may, for instance, be only one of the ways through which sex and family may be realized today. Nevertheless, the marriage celebration—for those who choose it— is a powerful symbol and should be a vital part of the Corporate Saint's function in the total society.

The Corporate Saint should see to it that funerals are reclaimed from the sterile funeral parlors that proliferate today. Funerals should once more become celebrations in which death, no less than birth, is recognized as a gift of life. Unlike baptisms (certainly adult baptisms) and weddings, funerals are not celebrations in the life of the individual whose life has come to an end. Instead, they are celebrations in the lives of those who know that their own lives are defined by death—and always have been. The Department of Transitions should, therefore, be extremely alert to deaths among the Secular Saints, in order to assist those who remain in celebrating the completion of life instead of allowing it to be the occasion for despair.

Personal counseling is a responsibility that many clergymen have gladly assumed in recent years, but it requires skills that not every staff member of the Corporate Saint may possess or wish to attain. It is entirely appropriate that this function should be specialized as are the other duties of the organization. The Department of Personal Counseling could easily become a full-scale counseling center, with a staff of trained psychologists who are Secular Saints. This department resides in the Division of Celebrations for the same reason that transitions rest here: personal crises are occasions for celebration of the limits and demands of life and must be received as such. Only when we can see crises in our lives as reasons for celebration are we able to praise God for *all* of life.

Social Action

The Division of Social Action is the intelligence arm of the Corporate Saint. Through its departments, it keeps a finger on the pulse of the service area, knowing where critical tensions exist within the body politic and feeding this information to the appropriate division or department of the Corporate Saint. It is also the direct-action arm of the organization, mobilizing persons within the area to take concerted action to correct flaws in the social structure by pressure upon the governments and businesses, which are the collectives that set the tone for the society as a whole.

The Department of Organizational Liaison is responsible for relating the Corporate Saint to all the collectives within the area, such as civic clubs, garden clubs, civic improvement groups, bridge clubs, labor unions, civil-rights organizations, Great Book societies, Welcome Wagons, and others. In cooperation with the Department of Personal Counseling, it identifies all the medical and social service agencies in the area and establishes connections with school administrators and teachers. Departmental staff actually become members of many community organizations and thereby facilitate the identification of Secular Saints heretofore unknown to the Corporate Saint, bringing the Christ possibility to them and their fellows. The Department of Organizational Liaison is the vital connective link between the Corporate Saint and every other collective in the area, without which the organization would be incapable of effectively performing its duty.

The Department of Governmental Relations is, as its name implies, the link between the Corporate Saint and the government or governments that have local jurisdiction. Modern society is conditioned by governments more than by any other single collective, a fact the Corporate Saint recognizes and takes responsibility for. Whether the government is municipal, county, state, or federal, it is the structure that develops the society-wide regulations that allow contextual freedom to its citizens, many of whom fall into the trap of assuming that nothing can be done to influence the nature of that freedom or (in some cases) bondage. The Department of Governmental Relations takes as its responsibility the task of ensuring that the right questions are constantly put to governments in order that the best interests of the people are served.

While governments have a tendency to assume a character of their own that is independent of the persons conducting them, those elected to public office are a matter of considerable importance to the populace and thus to the Corporate Saint. The Department of Governmental Relations formulates general policy, which is considered, amended, and adopted by the board of directors, relative to the positions on social issues and problems that appear to be most advantageous for the reception of the Christ possibility. The department then enters into the political arena, attempting to secure the election to public office of persons who hold these same policies. The Corporate Saint does not, of necessity, become thereby a political party, but it does actively endorse (as do newspapers and magazines) particular candidates, and works for their election. In this way it meets its obligation to do all within its power to guarantee a social context that eliminates the greatest number of roadblocks to the hearing and reception of the gospel. In politics, as in everything else, the Corporate Saint is concerned for only one thing: the Lordship of Christ.

The Department of Governmental Relations is equally concerned for legislation that is debated and passed by legislative bodies as it is for the election of Secular Saints to office. Thus, it keeps close watch on the United States Congress and state legislatures, and lobbies for legislation that is in keeping with its own goals and purposes. Administration of laws already passed is sometimes just as important as the passage of new laws, for administrative regulations have the force of law in actual practice. The department therefore establishes contacts with governmental administrators in order that the enforcement of laws may be in keeping with the Christ possibility, or at least not contrary to it. Part of the administrative mechanism is the police force, so the department maintains close contact with police and other enforcement agencies, constantly keeping the best interests of the people in mind.

In all its activity, the Department of Governmental Relations carefully develops relationships that facilitate trust in its judgments and that encourage public officials to seek its counsel as a representative of the people, a matter that is made easier by the work of the other departments of the Corporate Saint.

In American society, business and organized labor occupy a position of importance rivaling that of government. The Department of Business and Labor Relations is responsible for maintaining the same kind of relationships with this decision-making group that the Department of Governmental Relations is with governments. Staff of the department will become associates of key business and labor figures in the service area, constantly attempting to ensure the most favorable working conditions for employed persons and the equitable distributions of products and services. This department establishes and maintains the Corporate Saint as a respectable and influential collective among the economic community—and so facilitates the hearing of the Christ possibility by members of it, thereby benefiting all people of the area.

Probable Problems

A number of differences between the Corporate Saint and the parish church may appear as insuperable obstacles to the creation of a Corporate Saint in any given area. What about church membership? Will people be members of their local church or will they be members of the Corporate Saint? How will the Corporate Saint be financed? It looks as though all the work will be done by staff. What about member participation and the ministry of the laity? What happens to denominational affiliation of churches? Will they still be Baptist, Episcopalian, or Methodist?

No question about it: the widespread development of Corporate Saints will have a radical effect on church membership, financing, and denomination structure. But the effect will come by evolution and will cover a period of some years, making the shock and anxiety attendant upon revolutions far less acute.

The extent to which Protestantism depends upon membership in parish churches is remarkable in itself. Roman Catholicism has never had such a dependency, because of its insistence that it is the only Church. Protestantism, on the other hand, has recognized the plurality of contemporary society, and its membership structure reflects the fact that men and women may belong to a number of different groups, among them the church of their choice. Anyone may become a member of a Protestant church by declaring his faith in Jesus Christ and agreeing to abide (more or less) by the rules of the particular denomination. But everyone knows that there are at least two levels of membership: the nominal member and the "good" member. The nominal member has his name on the rolls, but seldom attends worship services, takes no part in parish activities, and, above all, makes no financial contribution. The "good" member, on the other hand, does all the things the nominal member does not do, particularly in the financial realm; the "good" member supports the church with his regular monetary gifts.

The Corporate Saint does not have individual members. In its initial stages, it is constituted by member churches, who elect persons to its board of directors, but individual persons are not members. Instead of members, the Corporate Saint has constituents, in the same sense that a senator has constituents—the people served by the organization, or who take advantage of the programs offered, or even who merely live and/or work within the geographical area to which the Corporate Saint directs its efforts.

The parish church (which does have members) is changed significantly through its decision to participate in the formation of a Corporate Saint, for the functions formerly performed by the church —Sunday schools, women's societies, worship services, social service projects, etc.—are now performed by the new organization. What is left for the parish church? Won't its members lose interest entirely?

Once it has placed its organizational activities in the hands of the Corporate Saint, the parish church is fast on the way to becoming a congregation of Saints. No longer does it seek out members, for membership is unimportant or nonexistent for a congregation. The number of people who are formally affiliated with the former parish church will doubtless drop, but the quality of the congregation will be enhanced; it will now become a group of Secular Saints who gather together occasionally for worship and fellowship, nothing more. As the parish church evolves into the congregation of Saints, it becomes less and less formal in structure, and fewer of its meetings are held in the church building (which is now devoted to the program of the Corporate Saint). It may very well split into several congregations, meeting when and where those who constitute it decide. No clergyman is required for these meetings, for the Secular Saints know full well that each of them is equally qualified to preach the Word and administer the sacraments.

Eventually the parish-church identity vanishes, at which time there will be no body to elect members to the Corporate Saint. But by this time, the Corporate Saint will have developed to a level where it will be self-perpetuating, electing its own board members as do the boards of corporations and other collectives in the society at large.

As it begins operation, the Corporate Saint will doubtless draw its financial resource from the parish churches that constitute it and from denominational boards and agencies that have funds for creative innovations within the denominational structure. But both of these sources will dry up as the parish church ceases to be a viable financial unit and the denominations, which rely upon the parish church for their funds, change in character. The Corporate Saint, therefore, will derive its monetary support from other sources. Prime among these will be its own operations. The school for continuing evangelism will bring income from tuition and fees, enough to support itself and then some. Weddings, funerals, and baptisms will be performed on a set-fee basis. Sizable financial sustenance should come from the large public celebrations conducted by the Department of Feasts, and admission fees to lectures, forums, etc. will further enhance the financial base. In addition, contributions will come from individual Secular Saints, solicited on the same basis as such organizations as the Heart Fund now solicit, and from business and industry. The Corporate Saint, once it has established itself as a genuine area-wide public service organization, should have little difficulty finding its financial base in the area it serves. In other words, it can find money if it does its job well. And if it does not do its job well, it deserves to die.

Although most Corporate Saints will probably begin as cooperative organizations of several churches belonging to the same denomination (it is easier that way; organic denominational cooperation is still very difficult), the organization should be completely open-ended, allowing for the incorporation of other denominational churches or more of the same denomination. As various churches begin to affiliate with the Corporate Saint, so do their denominations, in exactly the same way that some parish churches today are affiliated with more than one denomination. But when an organization recognizes a number of parent suprastructures, it becomes, in effect, autonomous. Thus it is with the Corporate Saint. Each Corporate Saint is independent, developing its own structure, its own program, and its own financial base. The denominational boards and agencies, after which the Corporate Saint patterns its organization, will begin to assume a role different from the ones they now play. These boards presently are of two types: those that service local churches in their educational and community service projects, and those that work directly beyond the local boundaries on national and international problems plus the traditional mission activity. The former type will diminish in importance. Corporate Saints, with their own staffs of specialists, will develop their own curriculum materials and education techniques. No longer will the canned material from the denominational boards be necessary. Already, some pastors and other Secular Saints in the local churches are discarding such materials (no matter how well planned and carefully written) in favor of literature and collections of literature developed to fit the local situation. Denominational boards of evangelism, which are usually geared to increase local church membership rolls, will become totally obsolete as the Corporate Saint, whose *raison d'être* is evangelism or Word-declaring, goes about its task without the benefit of membership. Agencies designed to enhance denominational financial structures will have a far easier job, because they will have fewer local units with which to deal, and much less money to handle.

The agencies that attempt to affect directly the national and international social structure, either by missionaries who establish congregations of Secular Saints or by influencing national and international public policy, will no longer be saddled with cultivation of the local parish church for emotional and financial support. They will become Corporate Saints in their own right, deriving financial support from other Corporate Saints, doing their assigned tasks independent of the local units, which have their own responsibilities.

By assisting in the development of Corporate Saints, bishops and others in the ecclesiastical oversight administration will work themselves out of a job, at which time they may move into the Corporate Saint as experts in their chosen fields. A bare minimum number of denominational administrators will remain to correlate the work of the national and international Corporate Saints, which will be financially supported by Corporate Saints who also support other such denominational agencies. The inevitable result will be a reduction in the number of denominations, which by this time will be so different from what we now know as denominations that the name will scarcely apply.

The Ecumenical Movement is presently moving in the direction of organic union of denominations with the expectation that this step will demonstrate the unity of the church. But the development of the Corporate Saint will obviate the necessity of the Ecumenical Movement by effecting union on a pragmatic basis at the local level. As the Corporate Saint evolves, the denominations will fade away to emerge as a few national and international Corporate Saints. Just as Ford, General Motors, and Chrysler see no need to merge into one gigantic corporation, so the denominations will see no need to merge into one church. The competition can be beneficial. The communion of Saints is no less one communion because several organizations exist to make the Secular Saint's mission concrete in history.

A final word: the Corporate Saint is autonomous, even though it may, for practical purposes, be aligned with a denomination. It does not follow any party line, but makes its own decision about how it will conduct its program, seeking the help it needs from whatever source is available. Just as the Secular Saint is an individual among individuals, so the Corporate Saint is an individual among corporations. It is free.

A SUMMARY NOTE

The Secular Saint, who lives as a free, responsible human being, who joys in every little bit of his life, worships and studies whenever he encounters another Secular Saint. But he knows that he cannot do the entire job of making the Christ possibility known to all parts of his relationship matrix, or self, alone. Therefore, he supports the Corporate Saint, the organization whose responsibility among other organizations is to make the Christ possibility available to society as a whole.

In every case, the possibility of relating to the absolute limits and impossible demands of life by receiving them as great, good gifts—the Christ possibility—is central for the Secular Saint. His every act, his every decision is taken within the context of that possibility, for Christ is Lord of his life.

The Corporate Saint is the organizational equivalent of the Secular Saint. Among organizations in this organizational world, the Corporate Saint acts as a free individual. Related formally for practical purposes to denominations and other collectives, the Corporate Saint moves within the geographical area it has chosen to develop social contexts in which the Christ possibility may be heard and received. In so doing, it remains autonomous, an individual organization, renouncing affiliations that would bind it to a particular set of study materials, a particular life-style. Before God *and men*, the Corporate Saint is free to do as it wills.

The affirmation of individuality made by the Secular Saint, as a lonely individual, and the Corporate Saint, as a lonely organization, is its declaration of freedom in Christ. It represents, also, its willingness to assume responsibility for its own life and the consequences of its actions—trusting always in the Word that clues it in that whether it lives or whether it dies, it is the Lord's (Christ's). Neither the Secular Saint nor the Corporate Saint fears for the future. Instead, they trust the future to be good, as the past (in faith) has been, and in that confidence they go about trying to wake people up to the goodness of their own lives, both personal and organizational.

Secular Saint, Saints together, Corporate Saint. Any man may be a Secular Saint without even being aware of it. Any man may be in communion with other Secular Saints, even over a business lunch. Any man may be a constituent of the Corporate Saint by participating in its program. Any man may acknowledge Christ as the operating mode of his life, his Lord.

IV

Reflections

8

Shouting Stones:
Notes on the Poetry

THE POETIC PROCESS

Faces I too have seen in clouds
And on the walls of an outhouse;
And this morning I saw a frog
Deadstill, showing its moist, grey
Belly to some twigs and dry straw;
And a young terrified grass-snake
That threw off M's and bright S's
At the exact ferns as it streaked
Across my black boot into sedge.

To begin with there are the
   mysteries;
Though Klee recommends
   character
And Maritain has one lattice
That gives upon a monastery.
They write well: moreover, Klee
   paints.
To make a distinction, I think
Then that the poet transfigures
Reality, but the traffic cop
Transcribes it into his notebook.

In any case I'm adjusting
My organs to the future. Lies?
No: Language. The great days of
   Liz
Are mere Marlovian bombast:
The truth is dung, bubonic plagues
And London a stinking midden;
The maids unwashed and
   credulous,
The men coarse, or refined and
   corrupt
Reading their folios.

Sure I've come upon calyxes
And calicos, and melonrinds,
And fruitstones that reminded me
Of the bleeding heads of soldiers;
I've sworn then by the blood and
   gall
Of Christ and shouted eurekas
Till seven beavers watered me,
Putting out the fires. I've prayed,
Prayed and wept like a lunatic.

So I come back to the white clouds
And the outhouse wall. One may see
Faces anywhere if one's not proud.
The big words? I'd rather find lips
Shaping themselves in the rough wood;
Or connect my manshape's shadow
Floating like a fish under me
With—fish! Or think the day closes
Like the sad, red eyes of your English cocker.

IRVING LAYTON

THE ARTIST is the man in any field, scientific or humanistic, who grasps the implications of his actions and of new knowledge in his own time. He is the man of integral awareness."[1] Marshall McLuhan's observation is, of course, nothing particularly new: for years men have been going about saying the artist represented the true barometer of any given age. McLuhan, in fact, acknowledges this by calling attention to Flaubert's declaration that "The War of 1890 need never have been fought had people read my *Sentimental Education*."[2] The problem precisely is that people do not read, or look at art, and no barometer is useful if it is not consulted.

An artist may or may not be a Secular Saint, he may or may not receive his limits and demands as good gifts, but he does recognize them for what they are: limits and demands. Picasso, for instance, viewed the first experiment in saturation bombing, the destruction of the Spanish town of Guernica, as a great, unmitigated evil, and his painting cannot be interpreted otherwise. Protest is one way to deal with existential limits, and can be a powerful avenue for affirming them. Affirmation does not always mean approval, but it does mean facing the limit openly and freely, which is just what Picasso did. The artist—when he is an *artist*, which only a few painters, writers, and composers are—tells us the truth about our world. And those with eyes to see discern that truth for what it is. The artist must be taken with utmost seriousness and his work carefully considered if we are to tie in with the God activity that surrounds us.

As a general rule, artists are no more reliable when they talk about their art than are other critics. In fact, they may be even less reliable, but an artist's observations remain instructive for what they reveal about what he *intends* to do, even if he is not capable of bringing it off or actually produces something else. In a fascinating discussion of contemporary art, *The Insiders*, Selden Rodman notes Beethoven's observation to an interviewer that music "is the mediator between intellectual and sensuous life . . . it is the one incorporeal entrance into the higher world of knowledge which comprehends mankind but which man cannot comprehend." Rodman then adds, "The point to note is that the supreme artist did not regard art as an end in itself but as a means of comprehending life."[3]

I have attempted to argue in the preceding pages that the Trinitarian symbols are means for comprehending life and, more than that, relating to life. More than happenstance is involved in the persistent interest artists have taken in religious subjects; art is drawn to Christian faith and Christian faith is drawn to art because each is concerned for symbolizing man's actual position *vis-à-vis* his world.

Rodman discerns an artistic movement whose practitioners he calls "the Insiders." While not members of a school, the Insiders share common life-understandings that are very similar to those of the Secular Saint, who also is not representative of any school or movement or cause. "An Insider," Rodman writes, "is an artist who feels drawn to values outside himself strongly enough to examine them in his work.

"Since 'values outside himself' is taken to mean concern with the human condition, the Insider expresses that concern in some form of representational imagery, or . . . in an aesthetic vocabulary evocative of that condition. . . . the Insider steeps himself in tradition, regarding his particular form of expression not as a defiance of the past but as a creative re-expression of the same aspirations."[4]

When the Secular Saint works at contemporary understandings of Christ, he is engaged in the task the Insider carves out for himself in art. As the artist's medium is paint or stone or language or music, the Secular Saint's medium is the historic symbolism of his faith. What he does with it is up to him. The following comment on the Insider could equally be made of the Secular Saint: "Believing neither in 'progress' (which assumes the inevitability of an unrealized and therefore abstract future) nor in 'reaction' (a return to other styles as exotic escapes from present reality), the Insider searches for images of truth that will be meaningful to his contemporaries."[5] The Secular Saint is not interested in abstractions so much as he is in concrete symbolic modes that actually make sense to his fellows. But the problem comes when he asks just who his fellows are. As I suggested in Chapter 1, any man may get stuck in a transitional period that has actually ceased to exist as a viable operating context, yet that makes him no less a contemporary of the Secular Saint. Apologists for Christian faith have always been concerned for those who are not up to stomaching symbolic modes of tomorrow's today. What about the person who actually finds significance in the stop-gap God? Must he be addressed in terms of that God? Both the Insider and the Secular Saint would have to answer in the negative, for whether we are aware of it or not, the stop-gap God is no longer a genuine possibility. What the Secular Saint attempts to do, however, is use the word God in such a way that it makes genuine contemporary sense *both* to the believer in the stop-gap God and to the man of religionless Christianity, and thereby to transform their stance toward life. The Secular Saint agrees with Rodman: ". . . the Insider believes that the full development of man (if man is to come to grips with himself as part of a total reality) requires the rational evolution of *both* thought and feeling."[6]

Luke's Gospel has some Pharisees approach Jesus. " 'Teacher,' they said, 'command your disciples to be quiet!' Jesus answered, 'If they keep quiet, I tell you, the stones themselves will shout.' "[7] Jesus' contemporary disciples, the Secular Saints, have been remarkably quiet in recent years, despite all the talk about a revival of religion. But the stones have been shouting, and the stones are the artists, among them the poets.

The shouting poets are among Rodman's Insiders, who may well be considered colleagues by the Secular Saint. The Insider is an individual and is concerned for the authenticity of the individual. "He never depicts misery in the mass, as does the Communist artist, because he conceives evil and redemption in personal terms, soluble only through the volition of the free spirit. . . . But in his search for values that give meaning to life, the Insider does not divorce man as an individual from man as a social participant. Machines employed for any other purpose than liberation enslave; and the State is to be tolerated only if it serves to distribute freedom."[8] The Secular Saint understands his position in life to be identical with that of the Insider. He, too, "seeks as much schooling as he can absorb. On the living body of the past, with love born of understanding, he endeavors to beget a style of his own. Failing this, he will not scorn to contribute his share of a dedicated craftsmanship, recognizing that without it tradition cannot be kept alive."[9]

Secular Saints are discriminating when it comes to artists. Generalizations such as McLuhan's are of only general value for them, because they assume that any person who paints a picture or composes a poem—particularly if he has been critically and publicly acclaimed—is pointing in the same direction the Secular Saint points. (Other artists may have *strategic* importance for Secular Saints because they offer opportunities to indicate false options toward human existence.) "To be great," Rodman quotes June Wayne, a contemporary printmaker, as saying, "one must feel pity on the mass level, and none for the individual. Otherwise, one's pity gets in the way, and one is captured and crippled." But, Rodman asks, "is not the measure of the Insider's greatness the extent of his capacity to be captured *without* being crippled?"[10] This is an exact statement of the Secular Saint's life-style. He does well to consider carefully the artists who fall into Rodman's Insider class. The poems affixed to most of the chapters in this book are such, and have been intentionally selected because each points to an aspect of the Secular Saint's understanding of the life of contemporary men and women.

"The Poetic Process"

Attempts by poets to comment on the meaning of poetry by means of poetry are properly suspect, for they are efforts to combine criticism with the medium being criticized. I do not think that Irving Layton, as revealed in his poetry, is an Insider, much less a Secular Saint, but I do think "The Poetic Process" can be of assistance toward approaching poetry in general and the other poems here under discussion. I do not propose to offer any detailed analysis of any of these poems—after all, they speak for themselves. Instead, I wish to suggest several general characteristics of each and call attention to certain portions that are of particular interest to the Secular Saint.

The poetry that talks to contemporary men of Christian faith speaks of everyday events in ways that allow those events to become revelatory of the character of all events. It does not limit itself to an interior world, but looks outward to a man's relationship with every part of his definition. Thus, Layton says that "the poet transfigures/Reality, but the traffic cop/Transcribes it into his notebook." Transfiguring reality is an awesome responsibility, the responsibility for providing symbols that allow human beings to appropriate reality. Whatever reality is, it cannot be apprehended through any mechanism other than the symbol, for a symbol is a conceptualization that holds in tension a great host of life's elements, setting them out before a man in such fashion that he can comprehend his life *in toto*, rather than fragmented as it actually comes to him.

We must not malign the traffic cop for writing reality in his notebook; after all, traffic tickets represent tangible encounters with God. But only the Secular Saint is able to identify the particular ticket with the absolute limits and impossible demands of his life. Nevertheless, poets take upon themselves the obligation to provide secular symbols by means of which the reality Secular Saints know as God may be revealed.

Layton says he is "adjusting/My organs to the future." More power to him! But what does that mean? It means he has chosen that the present will be conditioned by what is to come more than by what has already come. As the Secular Saint knows, the past must not be ignored; it must, on the other hand, be affirmed as good. Nevertheless, the present is not simply the predestined apex of the past, but is the creative interaction of the past and the future—as understood to be good through the Christ possible response to whatever has come or is to come.

The poem begins and ends with "Faces I too have seen in clouds/ And on the walls of an outhouse;". The Secular Saint sees faces, too; that is, he sees reality with which he can identify everywhere he turns. The clouds, the outhouse walls, the daily newspaper, the stream of morning traffic, the memo on his desk, the household cleaning present him with faces as he encounters his limits and demands every day. He is an integral part of everything in the created universe, nothing is alien to him, although everything remains, to some extent, "the mysteries"; never can he comprehend the complete meaning of what comes over his hill.

The Secular Saint, too, would "rather find lips/Shaping themselves in the rough wood;/Or connect my manshape's shadow/ Floating like a fish under me/With—fish! Or think the day closes/ Like the sad, red eyes of your English cocker." The poetic process is the process of tying in with the universe in its mundane, insignificant happenings—and finding the meaning of all life there.

With this preface, therefore, let us now turn to the Insider poems affixed to Chapters 1–7 and thereby recall the life of the Secular Saint in his symbolic and organizational existence.

"pity this busy monster,manunkind,"

e. e. cummings published "pity this busy monster,manunkind," in 1944, the year before World War II ended, but the poem talks to the emerging steady-state world of tomorrow's today as few really contemporary poems do. We are not to pity "manunkind," a made-word that transforms "mankind" into a moral judgment, for "this busy monster" plays games with the artificial world he has created. It is a world in which electron microscopes can make a God from the simplest everyday object and telescopes assist in proving Einstein's notion that space is curved, bringing the beginning of things right back to the present. In the midst of all this magnificence, man himself becomes an "unself" afflicted with the comfortable disease of progress.

Progress is a legacy left us by the Enlightenment. According to Peter Gay, "The theory of progress . . . gave formal expression to the hope that the alternations between the Ages of Philosophy and the Ages of Belief were not inescapable, that man was not forever trapped on the treadmill of historical cycles."[11] But cummings calls this theory "a comfortable disease" that ignores the realities of life and death in the effort to objectify everything, an effort that is finally destructive of the self. In the late 1960's we have discovered cummings to be right: progress itself leads us back to the Psalmist's question, "What is man?" The poet says, "A world of made/is not a world of born." We now suspect there may not be too much difference between the two worlds: creation of life in the laboratory is not far off. But birth is just infinitely different from building hearts and lungs; birth has to do with the emergence of the Secular Saint, with the appearance of men and women who approach their future with anticipation—no matter whether it come as pleasure or pain. Birth simply does not fit within the context of progress, in fact it goes counter to all progressive impulses and movements, because progress demands a sterile movement into the future that fails to take the limits and demands of life as anything other than obstacles to be overcome, while birth calls us to joy in our definitions, overcoming those we can and loving those we cannot.

The poem is not a comment upon microscopes and telescopes, upon modern technology in itself, but is rather an observation upon the character of the relationship men have with contemporary existence. The final words of the poem, therefore, may be taken in two ways. If the "universe next door" is a reference to the technological world, the poem is simple irony. There is no universe next door, and the poet knows it, just as he expects his hearers to know it. Still, we look for such an escape from the limits and demands of the universe we have on our hands, only to discover the new universe to be exactly the same as the first.

But the words, "We doctors know/a hopeless case if—listen:there's a hell/of a good universe next door;let's go," do not have reference to the world at all. Instead, they refer to man's relationship with the universe: it is "this busy monster,manunkind" who is "a hopeless case," not the technological world. He is hopeless because he lives in the "world of made," but he is not to be pitied, because, unlike animals and inanimate objects, he can choose how he will relate to the world he himself created. There really is "a hell/of a good universe next door"! It is "a world of born," in which no one need be a "fine specimen of hypermagical/ultraomnipotence." It is the world of the Secular Saint.

The cries of stones such as cummings' poem were desperately needed in 1944, when man was on the verge of destroying himself by waging the most vicious war in history, but somehow its words seem more appropriate for the 1960's, when man, particularly Western man, has placed his entire confidence in technology, especially what McLuhan calls the "instant speed" of electronic communication media. Our emerging steady-state world can be a "world of born" if we choose that it be so.

"A Refusal to Mourn the Death, by Fire, of a Child in London"

"A Refusal to Mourn the Death, by Fire, of a Child in London" may inappropriately be here labeled a shouting stone, for it comes quite close to being a direct testimony to Christian faith. The poem is, in fact, a remarkable combination of traditional Christian symbolism with wholly secular reality, in the process of which religious language becomes religionless and a legitimate part of everyman's speech.

The poet refuses to mourn a death, an act that is exceedingly strange in contemporary culture, especially a refusal to mourn the death of a child who had all of life before her. By such refusal, the poet ends up speaking of life far more than death. And he does so from a perspective shared by the Secular Saint. The poem is a celebration of God.

The word "God" does not appear, but the Secular Saint knows the symbolic name for "the mankind making/Bird beast and flower/Fathering and all humbling darkness," the beginning and the end, the absolute limits to life. If God "Tells with silence the last light breaking/And the still hour/Is come of the sea tumbling in harness/And I must enter again the round/Zion of the water bead/And the synagogue of the ear of corn" *then* the poet will mourn. The words associated with religion—"Zion," "synagogue"—are here taken out of their usual context in the Jewish faith and made to refer to "the water bead" and "the ear of corn." Both words suggest refuge: Zion the earthly refuge for which the Hebrew people hoped, as well as the heavenly home that is both beginning and end; synagogue the place of quiet prayer and worship. But these images are given by the poet to his mother's womb ("the water bead" and "the ear of corn"), to which he would need return if he is to "let pray the shadow of a sound/Or sow my salt seed/In the least valley of sackcloth to mourn/The majesty and burning of the child's death."

The child's death was "majestic" and "burning"; both words suggest radiance, wonder, or even praise. This death is wonderful and good because it is the final glow of life for the child. No need of funeral orations for her, for they would only serve to "murder/The

mankind of her going." Mankind is defined by death and that definition is good, just as the cross was received as good by Jesus, an image
that is conjured up by the poet's refusal to "blaspheme down the
stations of the breath/With any further/Elegy of innocence and
youth."

The little girl is buried deep in Mother Earth along with all those
who have lived before—and the "riding Thames" also refuses to
mourn. "After the first death, there is no other." The last line lets
us in on the secret we had suspected all along: the "first death" occurs the first time a man becomes existentially aware of his own
finitude, of the fact that *his* life is defined by *his* death. All deaths
that occur within his self after that time are no longer deaths, provided he has come to terms with the "first death." The poet can,
therefore, declare that mourning is appropriate only should the universe be destroyed and he be born all over again into a new world in
which the "first death" had not occurred. Clearly, the poet does not
expect that miracle to happen; for him there simply is no further
death, but only the joyful celebration of life with its proper definitions, birth and death.

Dylan Thomas put his finger squarely on a great truth about the
lives of all men in "A Refusal to Mourn." It is a truth the Secular
Saint knows in the core of his being, the truth that the limits and
demands of his life may be joyfully received and gratefully acknowledged through the verbal symbol "God," whereby death does indeed lose its sting.

Everyone reads poetry, approaches any art, through a set of presuppositions, a set of conceptual categories, which allow him to see
what he sees. The Secular Saint's conceptual categories vary as
much as do those of any other man, with the important addition of
the Trinitarian symbols, which allow him to tune in much contemporary art, such as "A Refusal to Mourn," that otherwise would
be completely beyond his ken. The reason, of course, is that God,
Christ, and Holy Spirit are verbal symbols of life's truth, which is
also the subject of art.

"dying is fine)but Death"

Though radically different in style and approach, Dylan Thomas' "A Refusal to Mourn" and e. e. cummings' "dying is fine)but Death" speak to much the same point. Each denies death power over man and each celebrates life lived in the face of death. The principal emphasis in the Thomas poem is on the limits of life and secondarily upon the Christ possibility, while the reverse is true of the poem here under discussion.

The main device used by cummings is the capitalization of Death while leaving all other words in the poem, including dying, in lower case. Death and dying are as distant from each other as day and night, although they both refer to the same concrete event. The difference between Death and dying lies in the symbolic value of the words, and at that level the vast gulf fixed between them becomes clear. The poet says straight out what he means by the two words: "dying is/perfectly natural;perfectly/putting/it mildly lively(but/Death/is strictly/scientific/& artificial &/evil & legal)." The difference, in the language of the Secular Saint, is the difference between the sin response and the Christ response to the absolute limits and impossible demands of life.

The New Testament is filled with life-death references. Jesus brings a dead girl to life and raises Lazarus from the tomb. In Acts, Peter performs resurrection miracles. And the resurrection of Jesus caps the entire series of episodes. When the healing miracles are added to the explicit resurrection stories, a good bit of the Gospel material turns out to be a testimony to the possibility of living in life rather than living in death. And the meaning of Death in the New Testament is exactly the same as its meaning in cummings' poem: Death is the refusal to receive every little bit of existence as a good gift and to joy in it.

According to the poem, Death is unreality, detached from the way things actually are, detached from life. Death operates by rules and regulations ("scientific" and "legal"); Death is phony and malicious ("artificial" and "evil"). As we have seen, the sin response to life participates in these same unrealities, operating by rules (e.g., the rich young man) and believing that justification comes from maintaining the proper façade.

Dying, on the other hand, is "lively," for dying is a natural part of the life process, the absolute definition of a man's life. cummings, like Thomas, celebrates the terminus of life, even going so far as to thank "god/almighty" for it—and that is as it should be, just as it is entirely proper to link sin with Death in the final line. Only two ways for relating to the definition of our lives exist: sin and Death or Christ and life—and here another stone shouts out the message. The decision is up to us.

"Song of a Man Who Has Come Through"

D. H. Lawrence's poem presents us with the difficulty of the Holy Spirit life that is joyful in the midst of ambiguity. As we have seen, the Holy Spirit is present in man's decision to say yes to the Christ possible response to the limits and demands (God) of his life, and in his specific action upon that decision.

The wind of the poem is not the wind of John 3:8 ("The wind blows wherever it wishes; you hear the sound it makes, but you do not know where it comes from or where it is going. It is the same way with everyone who is born of the Spirit."), which is a direct reference to the Holy Spirit. Lawrence's wind is known by Secular Saints through the verbal symbol "God," the absolute limits and impossible demands of life that bat a man back and forth as he moves into his future. All of us are subject to this chaos, this nonorder, that characterizes the personal and social context of our life.

Blown as we are by God, we are called to decide how we will be blown. Will we, as it were, blow back, trying to pretend the limits are not there, the demands are unreal—or will we allow ourselves to be "borrowed/By the fine, fine wind that takes its course through the chaos of the world"?

Being "borrowed" by God is far different from being God's puppet, with no control over one's own decisions, as the poetic images employed by Lawrence reveal. The poet declares that "If only I am keen and hard like the sheer tip of a wedge/Driven by invisible blows,/The rock will split, we shall come at the wonder, we shall find the Hesperides." The formal structure of these lines is identical with that of Peter's words in response to the question, "What shall we do, brothers?" "Turn away from your sins, each one of you," Peter told them, "and be baptized in the name of Jesus Christ, so that your sins will be forgiven; and you will receive God's gift, the Holy Spirit."[12]

In each case an action on the part of the hearer is correlated with a corresponding action on the part of the limiting and demanding activity. Nothing wishy-washy is implied in choosing to be "the sheer tip of a wedge," just as the repentance demanded by Peter is far from easy. Yet each formulation is an effort to conceptualize the appropriate action in response to God. Lawrence says that when he becomes "Like a fine, an exquisite chisel, a wedge-blade inserted" then "we shall come at the wonder, we shall find the Hesperides." The Hesperides, of course, is the garden in which grew the golden apples, sought as utopia by mythical Greeks. In traditional Christian categories, the Hesperides becomes heaven, or, in Peter's terms, the Holy Spirit.

As an "exquisite chisel," the poet joins the disciples who made the decision to adopt the Christ Word as the operating mode of their lives: he acts as though he were drunk. "Oh, for the wonder that bubbles into my soul,/I would be a good fountain, a good well-head,/Would blur no whisper, spoil no expression." He would, in other words, joy in the Holy Spirit life, standing accountable for his every word and action, that they be in harmony with the gift of jubilant life.

In the midst of this rejoicing, however, a knock comes at the door. "What is the knocking?/What is the knocking at the door in the night?/It is somebody wants to do us harm." Many Secular Saints can testify to the terror Lawrence expresses here. It is the terror that accompanies the suggestion of doubt in the decision for the Christ possibility, the terror that intrudes into previously unalloyed joy. As such, it is the subjective manifestation of unfaith that each Secular Saint knows is the story of his life. Who among us has not become frightened at the advent of a new awareness of absolute limits and that just at the moment when he is rejoicing in receiving those limits as good gifts? "It is somebody wants to do us harm."

The poet quickly recovers. "No, no, it is the three strange angels./ Admit them, admit them." In a short essay entitled "Life," Lawrence sheds a bit of light on these two lines: "Who comes, who is that we hear outside in the night? Who knocks, who knocks again? Who is that that unlatches the painful door? . . . There is an arrival in us from the unknown, from the primal unknown, whence all creation issues. Did we call for this arrival, did we summon the new being, did we command the new creation of ourselves, the new fulfillment? We did not, it is not of us. We are not created of ourselves. But from the unknown, from the great darkness of the outside that which is strange and new arrives on our threshold, enters and takes place in us."[13] Action on the decision to be "the sheer tip of a wedge/ Driven by invisible blows" is constantly subject to the appearance of strange knockings at the door, always subject to the necessity for remaking, as the unknown, as God, demands fresh affirmative responses.

Like the poet, the Secular Saint responds by admitting whatever comes at his door as good, fully aware that his security rests precisely in his definition, that whether he lives or whether he dies, he is always an important person: "Not I, not I, but the wind that blows through me!"

"We Are Transmitters"

The life-style of the Secular Saint could be characterized, in part at least, by the term "life transmission," for the Secular Saint participates in life joyfully. In doing so, he embodies the life possibility that is Christ, making it available to those about him.

In "We Are Transmitters," D. H. Lawrence declares that "As we live, we are transmitters of life./And when we fail to transmit life, life fails to flow through us." No one is *alive*, the poet is saying, unless his life is something to be handed out to others. Closeted, life dies. But how is life to be transmitted? This question is somehow irrelevant to the Secular Saint, because he knows that his offering of the Christ possibility is part and parcel of his living; it is the definition of Secular Sainthood, not something that is added on after he has become a Secular Saint.

The word that "as we work, we can transmit life into our work" is the exciting knowledge of the Secular Saint, who sees all around him the infusion of excitement into even the most ordinary and common things he does, even "a woman making an apple dumpling, or a man a stool." Life for the Secular Saint includes his relationships with all other persons and things, for they all form the definition of his self. Unable to isolate himself from the stools and apple dumplings, the happiness and pain of other people, the deliberations of governments and traffic cops, he gratefully receives them all—and so desires that all portions of his self be presented with the gift of the Christ possible response to life. The Secular Saint is a transmitter of life *by definition*.

Yet, the Secular Saint knows Lawrence is right: "giving life is not so easy./It doesn't mean handing it out to some mean fool, or letting the living dead eat you up." The Secular Saint's temptation is to become so consumed with giving away the life possibility that he becomes one of the "living dead," who are, of course, those who have chosen the sin possibility as the operating mode of their life. Their heart beats and they walk around, but they see every limit and every demand as a grave threat to their existence until proved otherwise, and even then they are suspicious. The Secular Saint simply refuses to give in to this temptation, affirming himself instead as an important individual, separate from the others who form his definition at the same time he is integrally related to them. Only by so doing is he able to transmit life to the persons and things about him. Involved he is with the elements of his world, but identical with them he is not. The "living dead," like the poor, are always with us, but the Secular Saint by being a Secular Saint nevertheless transmits the living Word to them, offering the real possibility of resurrection.

Giving away the Christ possibility "means kindling the life-quality where it was not,/even if it's only in the whiteness of a washed pocket-handkerchief." The Secular Saint is grateful for shouting stones, such as Lawrence's poem, that let him know without doubt that the everyday objects and events of his life are not exempt from the life quality—if he chooses them not to be. When handkerchiefs can sing of life, everything can shout the good news that all of life is very good.

"There Was a Man with Tongue of Wood"

The Secular Saint is an individual. I cannot make this point too strongly, for in no sense is the Secular Saint identified by his participation in any organization or movement or cause. His Secular Sainthood rests only in his acceptance of the Christ possible response to his life, nothing else. Herein lies the principal difference between the Secular Saint and all Christians who have preceded him. At various times in the past Christians could legitimately see themselves as local embodiments of the people of God, which provided them with individual meaning. No longer is this the case. Today, men of Christian faith identify themselves solely in terms of the Christ possibility, which allows them to live independent of any organizational entity called "church" or any of the euphemisms for it.

The Secular Saint is the man "with the tongue of wood." He sets out to "sing" in the world, attempting, like Peter, to spell out the Christ possibility in such a way that every man can comprehend it. But most of the time his words come out as babble, as non-sense. The Christ possibility simply does not seem to be a real possibility for most men and women. After all, how could it make sense to say that *all* things are good and to be received as such? Obviously, the world is filled with evil and pain and anguish. But is it? Only if we choose it so. And the possibility of choosing life to be good is the option offered in Christ, the option elected by the Secular Saint.

Since his life mode is difficult for most of his contemporaries to accept, the Secular Saint seeks out those who understand life as he does, he gathers with other Secular Saints that they may "sing" together. "But there was one who heard/The clip-clapper of this tongue of wood/And knew what the man/Wished to sing,/And with that the singer was content." Precisely so. The Secular Saint needs only one other who sings his song in order to know its validity. Does he even need that? Yes and no.

The understanding of an other and the reciprocal testimony of that other is absolutely necessary for the Secular Saint, because he cannot declare the Christ Word to himself, despite his heightened awareness of it; memory serves just so long and then becomes insufficient. At least one other Secular Saint is required for him to maintain the Holy Spirit life. But what about the Secular Saint who, no matter how much he clip-clappers, can find no other who knows what he "wished to sing"? Is he less a Secular Saint? By no means, and he has no excuse for living the life of a bug on that account. Books are available, the Bible among them, to declare the Word to him; he has only to seek them out. And then there are the stones crying all around. The tree stands as living testimony to the reality of life: it just stands there being, and by doing so declares that life may be received as it is. The traffic cop presents the possibility of saying yes or no to the limit. The call to a new job offers the chance of affirming the Christ as the Lord of life.

Nevertheless, the Secular Saint looks for other Secular Saints with whom he may celebrate the goodness of life in the Christ response, and in this association "the singer was content."

"Once I Saw Mountains Angry"

The complexities of the contemporary organizational world often appear to the Secular Saint as "mountains angry,/And ranged in battle-front." The American tradition that a man can, through his own industry and perseverance, carve out an empire for himself and his family—the political version has the poor, industrious boy becoming President—has long since passed from reality into romantic tradition. In a time that has decreed the death of the corner grocery store in favor of the national supermarket chain, the individual man of Christian faith has difficulty considering the possibility that he could create an organization designed solely to proclaim the Christ possibility. Certainly he has trouble believing he could build such an organization from scratch. After all, he is "no bigger than my finger," compared to the organizational monolith required to do the job.

Of course, the Secular Saint knows he is under no obligation to construct a Corporate Saint any more than he is under obligation to do anything else. But there are those among contemporary Saints who desire to make the possibility in Christ available in a formal organizational structure, knowing that such is necessary if the Word is to be made available to the society as a whole. These make bold to stand against the mountains, to build a Corporate Saint from the ineffectual community clubs known as parish churches.

No mountain is as "angry" as the present denominational preoccupation with the parish church as the basis for Christian organization. Appearing to many as the last bastion of the community, the parish church stands alone on the corner of a residential street, vainly lifting its spire toward a nonexistent heaven and calling into its fold each Sunday a devoted group of persons who, in their heart of hearts, have long since abjured the parish as a viable organizational pattern, but who long for the day when security could be found by retreating to the comforting message of world-escape known as religion. This nostalgia is sufficiently strong for the Secular Saint to despair of ever creating an alternative organizational structure—the Corporate Saint—that will effectively do the job that needs doing in the last half of the twentieth century.

Occasionally a group of Secular Saints do attempt to scale the mountain and begin an embryo Corporate Saint. Should a skeptical observer ask, "Will he prevail?" the answer is given in Stephen Crane's poem: " 'Surely,' replied this other;/'His grandfathers beat them many times.' " The grandfathers of the Secular Saint have indeed, "beat them many times." Saint Paul developed viable organizations called churches that grew to become the ruler of the world under the influence of St. Augustine's creative mind. Later, Martin Luther broke with the powerful medieval church (without intending to do so, at least in the beginning) and developed the more or less autonomous parish church. Other grandfathers, such as John Wesley, John Knox, the Campbells, even Joseph Smith, all to one extent or another prevailed against the organizational mountains of the church world. Curiously enough, almost without exception these grandfathers had no intention of starting new Christian sects—but they did because the necessity for organization was stronger than the desire to live free of structural encumbrances.

The Secular Saint learns from the lessons taught by his grandfathers; instead of breaking with the denominations, he works within their context at evolving the Corporate Saint as a fresh organizational pattern without outright destruction of the parish system, which becomes the Corporate Saint over a period of time without conscious discontinuity.

A mountain climber is challenged the most by a mountain that no one has yet scaled, for which there are no grandfathers. At the same time, every mountain is capable of change itself: rockslides create new obstacles, clouds cover unknown peaks. So it is with the Secular Saint who endeavors to bring a Corporate Saint into being. Although ecclesiastical organization has been altered in the past, the present offers a fresh challenge, a challenge that is hopeful because "'His grandfathers beat them many times.'"

Along with Crane, the Secular Saint can "see much virtue in grandfathers—/At least, for the little man/Who stood against the mountains." The Corporate Saint—the pinnacle of the mountain— is yet to be realized, but it is on the way (in a multitude of specific forms) because the Christ possibility continues to be present as the only genuine life possibility available for secular men and women.

NOTES

CHAPTER ONE

1. T. S. Eliot, *The Complete Poems and Plays*, 1909–1950 (New York: Harcourt, Brace and Co., Inc., 1930–1952), p. 56.

2. Ibid., p. 4.

3. "The Effects of Space Exploration on Man's Condition and Stature," *The Future of Religions* (New York: Harper & Row, 1966), p. 43.

4. Ibid., p. 45.

5. John R. Platt, *The Step to Man* (New York: John Wiley & Sons, Inc., 1966), p. 197.

6. Ibid., p. 200.

7. "What TV is really doing to your children," *Family Circle*, Vol. 70, No. 3 (March 1967), p. 98.

8. Op. cit., p. 202.

9. *Letters and Papers from Prison* (New York: The Macmillan Co., 1967), p. 178.

10. Ibid., p. 179.

11. Ibid., p. 202.

12. *The Redemption of the Robot* (New York: Trident Press Bk., 1966), p. 222.

13. Op. cit., p. 200. (Italics added)

14. Op. cit., p. 98.

15. *Understanding Media: The Extensions of Man* (New York: Signet Book, 1966), pp. 290 ff.

16. *Family Circle* (March 1967), p. 99.

17. "Marshall McLuhan," *Commonweal* (January 20, 1967), p. 425.

18. *Understanding Media*, p. 275.

19. Ibid., p. 276.

20. Op. cit., p. 189.

21. *Understanding Media*, p. 304.

22. Platt, op. cit., p. 197.

23. "The New Aristocrats," *Playboy* (March 1967), pp. 154, 156. (Italics added)

24. Op. cit., p. 200.

25. *The Sane Society* (New York: Rinehart & Company, Inc., 1955), p. 72.

26. Ibid., p. 73.

27. Op. cit., p. 422.

28. Goodman, op. cit., p. 158.

29. Op. cit., p. 209.

30. Ibid., p. 171.

31. *Radical Monotheism and Western Culture* (New York: Harper & Brothers, 1960), p. 118.

32. Op. cit., p. 204.

CHAPTER TWO

1. Bonhoeffer, *Letters and Papers from Prison*, p. 190.

2. Stephen Crane, *Collected Poems* (New York: Alfred A. Knopf, Inc., 1930), p. 71.

3. Genesis 2:19.

CHAPTER THREE

1. Cf. Søren Kierkegaard, *The Sickness Unto Death* (Garden City: Doubleday Anchor Book, 1954), pp. 184–94.

2. Romans 14:7–8.

3. Romans 1:18–25.

4. Luke 15:1–32.

5. Confessions, Bk. XII.

6. Acts 26:9–19.

7. H. Richard Niebuhr, *The Responsible Self* (New York: Harper & Row, 1963), p. 166.

8. Dietrich Bonhoeffer, *Ethics* (New York: The Macmillan Co., 1955), pp. 55 ff.

9. Cf. H. Richard Niebuhr, *Radical Monotheism and Western Culture*, pp. 100–13.

10. Ibid., pp. 143 ff.

11. John 9:1–41.

CHAPTER FOUR

1. Acts 2:1–4.

2. E.g., Mark 6:52, 7:18, 8:17–21, 9:10, 9:32; Matthew 13:36.

3. Acts 1:6. (RSV)

4. John 14:9.

5. Acts 2:38.

6. Mark 10:17–27.

7. *Ethics*, p. 217. (Italics added)

8. Ibid., p. 248.

9. I Corinthians 12:3.

10. Joshua 24.

11. Acts 2:38–39.

12. *Ethics*, p. 218.

13. Ibid., p. 217.

14. Bonhoeffer, *Letters and Papers from Prison*, p. 198.

15. This is not the place to quibble about marshes and such as that; we are dealing with the myth, the symbol, the meaning of the Exodus account.

16. Mark 4:41.

CHAPTER FIVE

1. I Corinthians 6:12.

2. Romans 7:12.

3. E.g., Romans 6–8; I Corinthians 3:16–17, 7:8–9; Colossians 3:2.

4. "The Grand Tour," *Horizon* (November 1959), p. 95.

5. Ibid., p. 96.

6. Quoted in *The Washington Post*, May 14, 1967, p. C-1.

7. "The Rout of the Classical Tradition," *Horizon* (November 1960), p. 20.

8. Romans 8:35.

9. *Letters and Papers from Prison*, pp. 201 ff.

10. The Chicago Theological Seminary *Register* (February 1961), p. 25.

11. Luke 17:10.

12. John 5:18, 17:22.

13. Exodus 3–4.

14. Most of the phrases usually cited as being unclear in these letters—"religionless Christianity," "world come of age," etc.—are actually not so fuzzy. The problem is not so much what Bonhoeffer meant by them, but what they might mean for men in a changed world twenty years later.

15. *Letters and Papers from Prison*, p. 209.

16. Ibid., pp. 209 ff.

CHAPTER SIX

1. Dietrich Bonhoeffer, *Life Together* (New York: Harper & Brothers, 1954), p. 23.

2. Mark 7:24–30.

3. Mark 4:9.

4. Romans 1:17.

5. Galatians 3:26–28.

6. J. C. Hoekendijk, *The Church Inside Out* (Philadelphia: The Westminster Press, 1966), p. 101.

7. Ibid., p. 81.

8. I Corinthians 11:21.

9. *The Redemption of the Robot*, p. 145.

CHAPTER SEVEN

1. *The New Creation as Metropolis* (New York: The Macmillan Co., 1963), p. 127. (Italics Winter's)

2. *The Step to Man*, p. 172.

CHAPTER EIGHT

1. Marshall McLuhan, *Understanding Media*, p. 71.
2. Ibid., p. 70.
3. Selden Rodman, *The Insiders* (Baton Rouge: Louisiana State University Press, 1960), p. 62.
4. Ibid., p. 4.
5. Ibid., p. 5.
6. Ibid. (Italics Rodman's)
7. Luke 19:39–40.
8. Rodman, op. cit., p. 63.
9. Ibid.
10. Ibid., p. 110.
11. *The Enlightenment: An Interpretation* (New York: Alfred A. Knopf, Inc., 1966), p. 33.
12. Acts 2:37–38.
13. *Phoenix, The Posthumous Papers of D. H. Lawrence*, edited by Edward D. McDonald (New York: The Viking Press, Inc., 1936), p. 696.

FOR FURTHER READING

I have chosen the books listed below with some care, attempting to call the reader's attention to material of fairly recent origin that speaks to the subjects treated in *The Secular Saint*. While I often have serious differences in opinion with the authors noted here, each makes a contribution to the emerging discussion about the Secular Saint life-style and action for which I am indebted. This brief bibliography, therefore, serves the double function of providing suggestions for reading and expressing my own gratitude.

CHAPTER ONE   THE WORLD OF THE SECULAR SAINT

Dietrich Bonhoeffer, *Letters and Papers from Prison*
(New York: The Macmillan Co., 1953).

    The person who wishes to understand contemporary trends in theological thinking should be thoroughly conversant with this little book. Written while its author was imprisoned as a consequence of his part in the resistance to Adolf Hitler, it is a collection of letters written, for the most part, to his friend and former student, Eberhard Bethge. Here Bonhoeffer speaks of his now famous "world come of age" and "religionless Christianity." Although written over twenty years ago, this book is the work of a man who would be, had he lived, in his late fifties today and thus at the peak of his creative powers. It has remained for others to work out the implications of his creative formulas, which speak directly to the world of the twentieth century's latter days.

Harvey Cox, *The Secular City*
(New York: The Macmillan Co., 1965).

    Utilizing sociological and theological formulations that have become part of the furniture of contemporary thinkers about Christian faith, Cox produced a fascinating study in praise of life in the modern city, affirming its freedoms and possibilities.

Marshall McLuhan, *Understanding Media*
(New York: McGraw-Hill Book Co., Inc., 1964; paperback: New York: New American Library, 1966).

    Occasionally a book appears that bids fair to change the way in which men think of themselves and their world. Such a book is *Understanding Media*, in which its author explores the nature and impact of contemporary communication media. Whether a given person can "tune in" to McLuhan or not, this book is signally important for informed conversation about to-day's world.

John R. Platt, *The Step to Man*
(New York: John Wiley & Sons, Inc., 1966).
     A biophysicist, Platt maintains that man's evolution is proceeding at an accelerating rate in social, intellectual, and technological realms, in the proc-ess of which man's own decisions about his destiny play an important role.

CHAPTER TWO   THE EDGE IS THE CENTER

Dietrich Bonhoeffer, *Letters and Papers from Prison*.
     Bonhoeffer's discussion of where he points—and where he does not point—with the word God have been most influential on my discussion of God, especially the letters of 30 April 1944, 25 May 1944, and 8 June 1944.

Gerhard Ebeling, *God and Word*
(Philadelphia: Fortress Press, 1967).
     In a brief essay (forty-nine pages), Ebeling suggests that "God" points to "a word event that is always already in full swing" (p. 28).

H. Richard Niebuhr, *Radical Monotheism and Western Culture*
(New York: Harper & Brothers, 1960).
     Niebuhr's concept of radical monotheism is one of the key contemporary sources for rethinking the Christian faith. While certainly not new or unique in Christian history, his statement makes absolutely clear that Christian faith can tolerate only one God, which makes sophisticated versions of dual-ism, even allegiance to such deities as the stop-gap and escape-hatch Gods, untenable.

Schubert M. Ogden, *The Reality of God*
(New York: Harper & Row, 1966).
     The essays in this volume, particularly the title essay, outline what Ogden calls "neoclassical theism," which attempts to wed existential theology with the process philosophy of Whitehead and Hartshorne. Ogden's constructive effort is a significant attempt to maintain the validity of genuine transcend-ence while retaining the necessary immanence demanded by contemporary men. While the casual reader may find this book hard going, it is well worth the effort.

CHAPTER THREE   RESPONSE TO THE LIMIT

Thomas J. J. Altizer, *The Gospel of Christian Atheism*
(Philadelphia: The Westminster Press, 1966).
     As one of the principal exponents of death-of-God theology, Altizer is concerned to clear the decks of a transcendent God in order that the im-manent Jesus may have free sway. He denies contemporary transcendence

completely, but does so at the expense of allowing the former existence of a transcendent God. The resulting metaphysical schema sometimes seems a bit strange.

Dietrich Bonhoeffer, *Ethics*
(New York: The Macmillan Co., 1955).

This penultimate work of the German theologian was compiled from notes by his friend and biographer, Eberhard Bethge, after the author's death. Incomplete and enigmatic at times, the discussion of Christ's role in man's life is highly instructive, although careful and perceptive reading is requisite to understanding.

H. Richard Niebuhr, *Radical Monotheism and Western Culture*.

Radical monotheism, according to Niebuhr, involves a correspondence between the "principle of being" and "the principle of value." As a formula, this understanding means that "whatever is, is good" (p. 32), the formula I have suggested is the content of the Christ possible response to the persons, objects, and events of human life.

Paul Tillich, *The Shaking of the Foundations*
(New York: Charles Scribner's Sons, 1952).

The sermon, "You are accepted," speaks of the Christ possibility as the Word: "Simply accept the fact that you are accepted." This excellent formulation is premised, however, on an understanding of sin as separation from oneself, others, and the Ground of Being, which appears to be less and less meaningful to contemporary Saints, who experience themselves as choosing not to accept their acceptance rather than being separated from anything. The sermon (and others in the book) remains most helpful, nevertheless, in thinking through the meaning of Christian faith.

CHAPTER FOUR   THE DECISIVE SPIRIT

Dietrich Bonhoeffer, *Ethics*.

In his section on "The structure of responsible life," Bonhoeffer offers one of the two most creative discussions of decision in responsibility and freedom of which I am aware. While the Holy Spirit is not mentioned as such, the Spirit as revealed in the New Testament is clearly the appropriate rubric under which to appropriate Bonhoeffer's analysis.

H. Richard Niebuhr, *The Responsible Self*
(New York: Harper & Row, 1963).

An essay in the appendix entitled "Responsibility and Christ" contains the other creative discussion of Holy Spirit activity. Of particular note is Niebuhr's treatment of accountability and freedom.

CHAPTER FIVE   THE SECULAR SAINT

Dietrich Bonhoeffer, *Letters and Papers from Prison*.

These letters have attracted wide readership in recent years, as much for what they reveal about the life-style of their author as for their stimulating content. Demonstrating as well as discussing the life of a religionless Christian, they are the primary source for men and women who, twenty-odd years later, struggle with how to be faithful and this-worldly at the same time.

Joseph Fletcher, *Situation Ethics*
(Philadelphia: The Westminster Press, 1966).

This book is a good example of a recent effort to rethink ethics in a society that has little use for rigid moral rules and regulations. Fletcher maintains that love is the only absolute law and that the widest possible distribution of love is the highest good. The final word is far from having been spoken on contemporary ethics, and Fletcher does not approach it. Nevertheless, his book is valuable reading for Secular Saints who continue to wrestle with their own decision-making process.

Eric Hoffer, *The True Believer*
(New York: Harper & Brothers, 1951).

While this work by a man who persists in working on the San Francisco docks while lecturing at universities in his spare time is more than fifteen years old, it remains one of the most fascinating studies of fanatical movements and their leaders ever published. The Secular Saint can find here a guide to the dangers he faces as he moves about our organization world, not to mention some of the most interesting reading he will come upon.

Schubert M. Ogden, *The Reality of God.*

The title essay contains an instructive discussion of the self. On this subject, see also H. Richard Niebuhr, *The Responsible Self.*

Ronald Gregor Smith, *Secular Christianity*
(New York: Harper & Row, 1966).

Like Bonhoeffer's prison letters, this book raises questions and offers suggestions that are not fully developed. Perhaps for that very reason it makes exciting, though at times frustrating, reading. Certainly it should be on any Secular Saint's priority reading list.

CHAPTER SIX   SAINTS TOGETHER

Dietrich Bonhoeffer, *Life Together*
(New York: Harper & Brothers, 1954).

This book—a definitive discussion of fellowship among Christians—has been mistreated by countless study groups and retreaters, who have used it to reinforce their longing for escape from the world they have on their hands. But when *Life Together* is read in the light of Bonhoeffer's later works, the relationship between them becomes clear and the apparent piosity disappears. Nevertheless, this book requires updating in a way that the letters do not.

J. C. Hoekendijk, *The Church Inside Out*
(Philadelphia: The Westminster Press, 1966).

The thought of this Dutch theologian has yet to be fully considered by the Americans who could benefit most from it: the "ordinary" layman and clergyman. This collection of essays is uneven in usefulness, but very suggestive of radical new understandings for Christian life in the world.

Martin E. Marty, *A Short History of Christianity*
(New York: Meridian Books, Inc., 1959).
A quick look at the history of the Christian community is important for those who would understand our present position in history. Marty's summary of church history is concise enough to suffice the nonprofessional theologian and offers a good backdrop for understanding what the Secular Saint rejects and what he accepts from his fathers.

George W. Webber, *God's Colony in Man's World*
(Nashville: Abingdon Press, 1960).
Growing out of his experience with the East Harlem Protestant Parish, Webber writes of "Christian love in action" in terms of the mission of the gathered people to serve the world. The emphasis is upon a remnant people who maintain themselves in faith by serious Bible study and worship while providing for the physical and spiritual needs of those around them. A pioneering work in the contemporary effort to understand Christian faith in modern society that is now of residual value.

CHAPTER SEVEN   THE CORPORATE SAINT

George W. Webber, *The Congregation in Mission*
(Nashville: Abingdon Press, 1964).
Many of the recent efforts to reconceive the church in twentieth-century America have centered on the inner city, where the ineffectiveness of traditional religious patterns has been most evident. As in *God's Colony in Man's World*, Webber here places emphasis upon the congregation as the renewing factor in the church. He has produced a suggestive book, based on the work of the East Harlem Protestant Parish, that nevertheless must be questioned in the light of a rethinking of theology and society. The book is part of the whole conversation about the social organization of contemporary Christian men that is still going on, and probably will continue to go on for some time.

Gibson Winter, *The New Creation as Metropolis*
(New York: The Macmillan Co., 1963).
Winter takes careful cognizance of the organizational character of our society and is much closer to my own position than is George Webber. He, too, sees the reshaping of Christian social organization to be centered in the city, and calls for the affirmation of various forms of ministry, particularly lay centers and training academies to replace local congregations. This book could profitably be read in conjunction with his earlier work, *The Suburban Captivity of the Churches* (Garden City: Doubleday & Company, 1961).

The Church for Others
(Geneva: World Council of Churches, 1967).
Here are recorded the reports of two study groups, one from North America and one from Europe, on new shapes of mission for the congregation. The

studies are particularly interesting as examples of ecumenical thought about the revolution now taking place in church life and the possibilities being considered by major church leaders on both sides of the Atlantic.

CHAPTER EIGHT   SHOUTING STONES: NOTES ON THE POETRY

Books of criticism from a theological perspective have proliferated in recent years, and the temptation to list those that have been important for me is great. But criticism is not the mode of the Secular Saint today, who asks only what art (including cinema) and literature says to him. I have chosen, therefore, to limit reference here to the following, which should be sufficient to suggest more than whole hosts of academic studies could possibly do.

Selden Rodman, *The Insiders*
(Baton Rouge: Louisiana State University Press, 1960).

LINCOLN CHRISTIAN COLLEGE AND SEMINARY

261
B864

79532

DISCARDED FROM
THE MILWAUKEE
PUBLIC LIBRARY
NOT FOR RESALE
OR RENT